HE SPOKE TO THEM
IN PARABLES

Other Books by Harold A. Bosley

THE QUEST FOR RELIGIOUS CERTAINTY

THE PHILOSOPHICAL HERITAGE OF THE CHRISTIAN FAITH

ON FINAL GROUND

MAIN ISSUES CONFRONTING CHRISTENDOM

A FIRM FAITH FOR TODAY

THE CHURCH MILITANT

PREACHING ON CONTROVERSIAL ISSUES

WHAT DID THE WORLD COUNCIL SAY TO YOU?

SERMONS ON THE PSALMS

SERMONS ON GENESIS

DOING WHAT IS CHRISTIAN

He Spoke to Them in Parables

HAROLD A. BOSLEY, Ph.D.

HARPER & ROW, PUBLISHERS

New York, Evanston, and London

To Margaret
whose love never fails

CONTENTS

vi   CONTENTS

PREFACE

Jesus of Nazareth was standing in a great tradition when he spoke to the people in parables, for parable has been the stock in trade of teachers of religion as far back as written records go. It is the skill and power with which he uses them that sets his parables in a world apart from others. He brought parable to a point of perfection that is perfection itself.

A word about parable as a literary form may be in place here. It is not to be confused with fable, simile, metaphor, or allegory—all ways of expressing likeness. In strict fact, parable "is a story that is or may be true to fact and is used generally to teach some moral or religious truth." Parable is not the oracular utterance of the inspired prophet streaked with vivid denunciation and highly emotional periods. Nor is it the deft sparring of the logician seeking advantage, if not victory, in the highly technical game of meaning. Parable is quiet, earnest conversation. It is a teacher explaining a point to a listener.

Jesus uses this honorable yet highly specialized mode of teaching as the most effective way of presenting important truths about God and His claim on man. By means of it, he reaches the heart as well as the head of mankind. Not for him the special language of the scientist, philosopher, or theologian. His parables are of the earth earthy even though he speaks of divine things. He uses the common tongue and homely, believable incidents drawn from daily life to interpret the ways of God to man. It is part of his mastery of parable that the God-ward look and lift of each story comes surging to the fore with such force that we almost forget the incident which brings it to us.

Clearly, one who speaks in parables must have a firm grip on the human aspect of the experiences he intends to use in this way. Jesus is always blending two worlds: the human and the divine. His parables are windows through which we view, first, a landscape with live people moving about on it, then, almost simultaneously, the vast new horizon of God's will enfolds and includes the human one. First we see a shepherd searching for sheep, then, in, through, and beyond it, God searching for men. All this with never an argument or appeal to reason—but the argument is unanswerable and the appeal inescapable.

vii

We are so familiar with some of the parables that it comes as a shock to realize that we are not able to determine the exact number of parables actually recorded in the Gospels. Scholars lead the chorus of uncertainty at this point with their estimates ranging from thirty-three to seventy-nine! Only nine parables appear in more than one Gospel, with six of these appearing in three Gospels—Matthew, Mark, and Luke. Each of these Gospels has some parables that appear nowhere else: Matthew has eleven; Mark three; and Luke fourteen. John, while alive with similes, metaphors, perhaps even allegories, has few parables. Some parables—the better-known ones—are fully developed stories; others are limited to a word or a phrase. Some scholars count all these as parables; others distinguish between parables in embryo and fully grown ones. Hence the difference between and among the scholars on this point.

But whether the parables appear one or three times, they have the effect of throwing open the windows and souls of men toward God. They probe the conscience, stir the emotions, and challenge the minds of men today as truly as ever.

No man can write in this field without acknowledging heavy debt to Dr. George A. Buttrick's great book, *The Parables of Jesus*—and this I do gladly. I have made extensive use of *The Interpreter's Bible*, the *International Critical Commentary*, the *Moffatt Commentary*, and the New Testament Commentaries currently being published by Harper & Row.

I have shared my enthusiam for the parables of our Lord with every church I have had the privilege of serving: Mount Vernon Place Methodist Church of Baltimore, Maryland; First Methodist Church of Evanston, Illinois; Christ Church Methodist of New York City. Student groups across the country have responded to them with genuine interest.

I am indebted to my secretary, Mrs. Robert Zeiller, for the typing of the manuscript and to my son, Norman, for a careful reading of it. I dedicate this book to my wife with the humbling awareness that no book of mine will ever be worthy of her name on the page of dedication. The subject matter of this one alone leads me to dedicate it to her since her life, like a parable, is a wonderful blending of the human and the divine.

Harold A. Bosley

Christ Church Methodist, New York
February 1, 1963

1. The Old Versus the New

LUKE 5:29-38*

I

One of the oldest problems men face is the tension between the old and new. We see it wherever we look in the human enterprise—whether in history books or in the unfolding issues of our time. "Yet why should this be so?" we ask. "Are not the old and the new inseparable in God's economy?" They seem always to exist side by side; they impinge on each other—sometimes in collision and conflict, sometimes in co-operation and peace. They may be likened to the two hands of God in the creation and control of this world of ceaseless change, of life and death. If we lived in a different kind of world, say, a wholly static one, one hand might do; but in this world, where life flows steadily through birth, maturity, and death for all living things, both old and new are needed and cannot be separated.

One such collision is written across every page in the New Testament, and we who are members of the Christian Church ought to be tremendously concerned about it. The people who gave Jesus the most trouble were the religious leaders of his people. Luke gives us this cryptic account of one such encounter and our Lord's reaction to it. Jesus was speaking to the scribes and the Pharisees and "he told them a parable also: No one tears a piece from a new garment: If he does, he will tear the new, and the piece from the new will not match the old.

"And no one puts new wine into old wineskins; if he does, the new wine will burst the skins and it will be spilled, and the skins will be destroyed. But new wine must be put into fresh wineskins" (Luke 5:36-38).

* All biblical references are to the Revised Standard Version unless otherwise specified.

1

Jesus had been trying to interest the scribes and the Pharisees in the great new fact of the kingdom of God. But they brushed this aside; they wanted to argue the pros and cons of fasting and correct ceremonies. He was stunned by their attitude. He saw in a flash their real tragedy: They had outlived their usefulness in the unfolding work of God. Speaking more in sorrow than in anger, he said with utmost simplicity: "God cannot use you in the building of His kingdom. You are blinded by your conceit; stifled by your righteousness; so enslaved to your way of doing things that God cannot get through to you with anything new or anything more. He cannot get you even to hear of the kingdom, let alone volunteer to serve and share in its coming."

What a fearful judgment to pronounce upon the accepted leaders of his people! But, in faithfulness both to his work and to their attitude toward it, it had to be said. Yet, Jesus could not have said it easily. For he was well acquainted with the glorious record written by the Pharisees over the preceding two hundred years. They had been strong, courageous, faithful, sincere leaders of their people. They had been the rock against which the Persian, Greek, and Roman despots beat in vain as they tried to enslave Israel. They had been the ones who fought to the death for their right to worship God—and they had won the victory for all.

Yet Jesus saw and said that while God might have used them in the past, He could not entrust to them the creation of His great new kingdom. Why? *They had lost the spirit of their faith in the forms of that faith.* They could not believe in the sincerity of anyone who differed from them in the little things: who did not fast, who ate bread without the ceremonial cleansing of hands, who had fellowship with sinners, who gathered food on the Sabbath day—or did anything else at variance with the laws of the Sabbath.

Jesus saw that God could not use such men because the wall of convention around their faith quite literally separated them from the world. Not only could nothing get in to corrupt their faith, but it was imprisoned there; it could not get out in service to anyone or anything outside. They simply could not be expected to hear and carry the Good News of the new gospel to the ends of the earth and assume the hard new work of sharing it with all of God's children. This task must be given to someone else, someone new to the trust of religious leadership:

to the sinners, the tax-gatherers, the artisans and fishermen, the common people. To such our Lord turned—and they came through beautifully!

II

Before moving to the areas of life where the old and the new are in conflict, we ought to note those where the old welcomes the new.

Not long ago, I had a conversation with a young chemist who had just taken a job with a great industrial concern. When I asked what he would be doing, he replied, "I will be working with a group without a definite assignment." "But what are you supposed to be doing?" I wanted to know. "Come up with something new—some new technique, some new process, some new product—perhaps a new industry," he answered.

This called to mind the man who had perfected a certain process in the manufacture of pigments. In the twinkling of an eye, he had rendered obsolete millions of dollars worth of newly installed equipment in the plant of his employers. He could not have destroyed the usefulness of that equipment more effectively if he had planted charges of dynamite throughout the plant. But did the company fire him for what he did? Hardly! They made him a vice president!

Science, industry, and business are looking for men with, or with the promise of, new ideas. That is why they are and will continue to be the driving forces of the modern world.

III

Would that a similar friendliness to new ideas and change could be found throughout life! But we find the old and the new locked in almost ceaseless conflict everywhere else we turn: home, government, and religion. Here the old not only does not welcome the new; it will strangle it in its cradle if it can.

Every parent faces or has faced this tension. Our most trying problem is not loving our child; or giving him proper nurture; or teaching him good manners. It is in knowing how and when to let go of him; to let him do his own thinking—and respect it; to make his own decisions— and to honor them; to make his own mistakes—and resist the temptation to say, "I told you so."

I confess that if there were in existence a scale which would tell a parent exactly how and when to do this, I would have purchased it long ago and used it night and day over the last decade or so. But, in simple truth, there seems to be no one way and certainly no easy way in which to let go of our children. Of this we may be sure: It could begin much earlier and proceed with a great deal more peace and joy than most of us realize. We could begin training our children in the disciplines of freedom almost as soon as they are able to walk. Then it would be easier to accept their later adventures in tastes, values, choices—perhaps even in popular music! It will always be hard to see them leave home for school or to set out for themselves in their own home and work, but it can be much easier on both parent and child than it usually is. And it would be, if the old would deal with the new in kindness and confidence.

Similarly, one of the basic problems in our form of government is in the relationship between the old and the new. Given a growing nation in a changing world, can a sensible person foresee anything more or less than continuous change in fundamental policies and institutions? Whether we like it or not, that is exactly what we have been witnessing all over the world for the last half-century and nowhere more concretely than here in the United States.

Many changes have been introduced in our way of life of late. Not all of them will survive; perhaps none will survive as they are—but it is now quite clear that many are going to be around a long time—at least until they are displaced by some newer development. The rise of labor unions, to cite but one example, has brought a new fact in the field of industrial life and thought—and it is here to stay. The development of governmental concern for equal educational opportunity for all children is shaking our entire public-school structure. Businessmen know of the many changes government regulations have introduced in their life and affairs. We may moan about them, but does anyone really foresee a time when the clock will be turned back to where it formerly was? Not even conservative leaders in business think this!

A distinguished gathering of business and professional leaders met in Philadelphia sometime ago and attempted to forecast what lies ahead of us for the next fifty years. They agreed on three things: (1) we face a strange period of change and expansion in every area of life; (2) it will be a period of untold danger to all men; (3) it will be a period when Christian idealism must guide the thought of men of business and industry if we are to survive.

They saw clearly that the forces behind the changes in our day are too deep-lying and too powerful to be denied some form of expression. We are caught up in "the wave of the future," and if we are wise we will seek how to go with it.

IV

But it is when we turn to the conflict between the old and the new in the field of religion that I confess to acute alarm. I should have been prepared for it since, years ago, I read and remembered Alfred North Whitehead's observation that while science places a premium on change and rewards it, religion is afraid of change and penalizes it. I did not want to believe it then, nor do I now. Is it true that religious institutions and religious-minded folk have been and are the last stand of reactionary conservatism? If it is true, then must it necessarily be true that religious organizations have usually been the stronghold—even the final stronghold—of the old order which is fighting vainly to stay the coming of the new? This was true in early Israel. Name any one of the great prophets —Isaiah, Jeremiah, Amos—and you have named a great rebel against the status quo in the religious and social life of his day. Imprisoned, threatened, and exiled by the powers that controlled things, they nonetheless stuck to their job. They were the new; and while what they represented could be hindered by the antagonisms and oppositions of the old, it could not be denied. The Lord of history saw to that!

Jesus found it to be so—as we have seen in his encounters with the scribes and the Pharisees who followed him, hoping to discredit him in the eyes of the ordinary people who were listening to him. They would not hear him out in what he had to say. The moment he criticized hallowed belief and custom, they blacked out. Their minds were made up; he was dangerous; he had to be silenced one way or another. They were the ones he had in mind and perhaps in direct view when he said, "You have eyes, but see not; and ears, but hear not." And so it went throughout his public ministry as he sought a hearing for the new among the custodians of the old. He saw that they would not listen; he saw the futility of expecting old wineskins to contain the ferment of the new kingdom of God.

Nor would the old wineskins of Judaism hold the new wine of Paul's faith in Jesus Christ. For the first half of Paul's public ministry, he fought the battle for freedom in the synagogues in the major cities of

Asia Minor and even in Rome itself. Though he and other Apostles fought a good fight, they lost on this point—and finally had to admit defeat. The old expelled the new; Judaism disowned the Christians, and the Christian Church was forced into being.

The old wineskins of the medieval church could not contain the new wine of the Reformation, though both Luther and Calvin tried to stay within the church. The old wineskins of the eighteenth-century Church of England were not able to hold the new wine of the Wesleyan movement, though Wesley, unlike the earlier Reformers, was able to stay inside the Established Church. He was so determined about it that he permitted no move toward separation as long as he lived. But he was hardly buried before his followers accepted the fact that they had been expelled in spirit if not in name from the church of their fathers, and set up one of their own.

V

The struggle between the old and the new keeps breaking out in the life of any church. A valued member of the church I once served was a man who prided himself on belonging to a manufacturing firm that was always bringing new developments into existence. He delighted in telling me how many millions of dollars the company poured into the processes by which such new articles were developed. Yet, believe it or not, when the Revised Standard Version of the Bible was placed on the market, his indignation knew no bounds. He opposed it in principle and any use we proposed to make of it in the Church School.

I tried to get through to him with the view that we needed to move in the direction of using the new translation. I started at the point where I thought I could touch him most quickly and deeply, namely, the cost of it—half a million dollars! That sobered him—but only for a moment. So I proceeded to tell him that it was easily the most accurate translation we have, and explained that competent scholars had made it from the best manuscripts available. But when my apologia for it was over, he shook his head sadly and said, "I like the King James Version, even if it isn't as accurate as this new one." And he never surrendered his conviction, even though the church went right ahead to use the new one.

A living church, a vital church, a growing church, is one that changes its program and form of witness, not in order simply to be changing but the better to serve the needs of the day to which it ministers. If two thousand years of Christian history mean anything at all, there is no stopping this process of change, nor should there be any desire to do so.

The longer I work in the Ecumenical Movement—which William Temple called "the great new fact of our time"—the more conscious I am of this upsurging of divine purpose, bursting old forms and creating new ones. The old wineskins of our separate denominations can no longer hold the new wine of the one great church in which we all believe and for which we seek to work. No one can foresee the end result of the changes now beginning to stir in our life and thought. The process had started, and in the providence of God it will continue until we have been brought more and more closely together.

There is something bigger than our separateness, and that something is the will of God whom we seek to serve. It will be a sorry day for the Christian Church if the scribes and the Pharisees among us, that is, the leaders of the churches today, seek to deny the full development in our life and time of this great new purpose of God in and through the churches. As surely as we are guilty of trying to do that, we will hear the voice of one of old saying again, "God can't use you. You have eyes, but see not; and ears, but hear not; and hearts, but feel not the deep pulsings of God's purposes."

VI

I do not blame the scribes and the Pharisees for loving and believing in the customs and beliefs that had stood the test of hard times. Nor do I blame them for thinking that they were honor-bound to protect these beliefs and customs against all critics who would seek to change them. I do not blame them for questioning and testing Jesus or any other person who seemed to be treating the time-tested institutions of religious faith lightly.

But I can and I do blame them for not giving Jesus Christ a careful and a fair hearing. I can and I do blame them for refusing even to face the meaning of the kingdom of God which he was announcing to them and seeking to interpret for them. I can and I do blame them for succumbing to the fatal temptation of believing that God could work only through them as they were! Surely the ultimate in self-righteousness has been reached when a group thinks God has reached a point of perfection in it which does not admit of further change!

I can and I do blame the scribes and the Pharisees of that and every other generation for the greatest mistake of all: They failed to distinguish between changes due to attack from the outside and changes due to pressures from deep within their own life and faith. If Jesus had been a Greek, a Persian, or a Roman seeking to root out Jewish customs and ideas, I could understand the way in which they closed ranks and removed him from the scene. But he was a Jew and carefully schooled in his and their heritage of faith. He was not an outsider; he was an insider. The suggestions he was making came from the heart of the Psalter, and the prophets, even from the spirit of the law of Moses—and the scribes and the Pharisees completely missed this point. Failing to distinguish between these two sources of change, they sought to expel anyone who tried to make any alteration in the status quo.

VII

The real issue must be faced by churchmen. Whose disciples are we anyway? Are we disciples of the scribes and the Pharisees? Or are we disciples of Jesus Christ, Paul, and the other great spirits of our religious tradition? This is not an idle question. It goes to the very heart of what we conceive our role to be in the church, in America, and in the world generally.

Let us be crystal clear on this simple fact: We cannot stop change; the new will come because it must come; God has written that into the basic law of His purposes for this universe. The new must come and the old must prove it, and having proved it, must yield to it. Then the *new* new becomes the old and waits for the next new to come surging up from the mysterious depths of God's creative purpose for life. And there is nothing we can or should want to do to change that.

Some years ago, we decided to purchase a film for showing at children's parties in our home as a way of maintaining a semblance of order and preserving the property. So, in searching out a proper film, I settled on one entitled, "The Birth of a Volcano." Let it be noted that this volcano really erupts! It is as awesome a sight as you will want to see.

The first time I exihibited the film to a group of boys, they were impressed, to say the least. So much so that one said in an awed voice, "How do you stop that volcano?" While conscious of the compliment he paid in thinking I might be able to stop it, I told him that we had never found out how to cap a volcano. If I were a Texan, I might try it, but being from a farm in Nebraska, the only thing I know to do when a volcano erupts is to stand clear and let her blow!

There is something of the inevitability of the eruption of a volcano in the great changes that have made and remade our religious heritage. No man has started them—though many have figured in them, and no man can stop them. We can delay, even distort them by our opposition and refusal to understand and co-operate with them, but we cannot deny them some sort of definitive expression in our common life. The scribes and the Pharisees could be instrumental in nailing Jesus to the cross, but they could not stop the preaching and the coming of the kingdom of God in the thought and the affairs of men. Nor can we —no matter how sincerely we may try!

When Pastor Robinson of the Pilgrim Fathers was strengthening them for the long move from Holland to an utterly new world and nerving them up to the task of starting life all over again under desperately difficult circumstances, he said something we need to take as nourishment for our spirit, "God hath yet more light to break forth from His Word." This word of blessing with which he sent the Pilgrims on their way comes from the very depths of God's continuing work in His world in our time.

2. The Power of Small Things

MATTHEW 13:31-35; LUKE 13:18-20

I

It will not be necessary to argue the power of small things to people who live, as we do, under the shadow of the atom. Even though we are told and try to believe that the atom is the great blessing for which we pray, we dare not forget for a single moment the threat which it contains. Too small to be seen by the naked eye, it is not too small to be known, respected, and feared by every sensible person. Indeed, as no other generation before us, we are or ought to be acquainted with the power of small things. Yet we are not the first to discover their power.

Jesus of Nazareth was acquainted with it, though for far different reasons. His parables of the mustard seed and the leaven suggest those reasons. Both are short—the one of the leaven taking twenty-four words —and they make the same point.

One parable tells of the swift growth of the mustard tree from the smallest of seeds to great height and luxuriant foliage. The other tells of the way leaven permeates the meal used in the baking of bread. Both parables dealt with things that every listener to our Lord had seen every day of his life. The mustard tree flourished in all of the valleys of Palestine. And it was alive with birds feeding on its seeds—perhaps within easy view of the ones who listened to this sermon. Bread was baked daily—sometimes for each meal—and leaven was needed for it, except on special feast days when unleavened bread was required by law.

Not many of us have seen a mustard plant. We are children of another age so far as the use of leaven in baking is concerned. We live on either bakery bread or these prepared mixes that have within them so remarkable a collection of ingredients that a cautious person cannot help wondering about the wisdom of eating them.

I do not know what doors this parable opens in your storehouse of memories, but it takes me back to early boyhood days on the farm in Nebraska and especially to that magic day each week when mother would bake bread. All our play was either discontinued or kept within easy smell of the kitchen. And as the odor increased, the players drew closer and closer to the door that had to be all but locked against us if any work was to be done inside. When the bread was done, and the six or eight golden brown loaves were put on the table to cool, we were admitted and permitted to stand around the table. As I recall it, the heat of our hunger went up in inverse ratio to the rate at which the bread cooled to where it could be cut, buttered, and consumed.

There was one mysterious aspect to that day which puzzled me then and has to some extent ever since—and it was called "the starter." This was some yeasty stuff, kept in a jar lowered in a wire container deep in the well to keep cool in the summer. If anything happened to "the starter"—it could go dead, grow sour, or the jar be broken—off we went to the neighbors to borrow some more. Since it was necessary to the baking of bread, Homer's Apollo of the winged feet never went more swiftly on an errand for Zeus than we went for "the starter" when told to do so.

I recall questioning and cross-questioning everyone concerned, especially Mother, about this thing, and getting no answer that would fit a five-year-old mind. But with or without an explanation, I could see the results. Without it a big pan of flour and water would be and remain paste. I knew, because I had tried it. But with a little of that mysterious ingredient called "the starter" the same pan of paste would begin to heave, toss, grow, and bulge in an awesome way. Paste became dough and dough became bread—at which point my metaphysical speculations gave way to a far more filling pursuit.

I like to think that Jesus was one of the millions of the children of the world who crowded around their mothers on baking day. I am sure he observed everything that went on with eyes that missed no move and a mind that sensed every meaning in it all. But on the occasion of some family feast he saw Mary prepare an unusually large amount of food. She took three measures of wheat—about one and one-half pecks in our measure, or over a quarter of a bushel—and put a little leaven in it, and it leavened the entire amount!

Apparently the leaven could act up then as later; could go sour and

spoil the meal even as it worked on it. When that happened everything had to be thrown out and a new start made all the way around.
Jesus had that in mind when he warned his disciples to "beware of
the leaven of the Pharisees" which he felt was corrupting religion by
reducing it to form and ritual. They spoiled everything they touched
because they themselves were evil, he concluded.

How richly our Lord was to use these experiences later when he
wanted to tell his disciples of the kingdom of God, of their role in its
growth, and of what it would mean to them and to all men. *He saw
in the leaven or yeast which Mary thrust into the kneading trough
filled with wheat or barley flour the kingdom of God being thrust into
the world by God through him and his disciples.* Few though they
were in number, and unimportant in influence or power, yet through
them the entire family of mankind was to be molded and shaped by
the power of the kingdom of God.

Jesus knew and believed in the power of small things. He is saying
three things in this parable: (1) small things can transform large ones;
(2) time is required for the transformation; (3) someone must do it,
and must know what he is doing and believe in it completely.

II

Most of us have learned never to underestimate the power of small
things, at least in some areas of life. I am impressed with the truth of
the parable each time we have the pleasure of giving a tea or a party
in our home. To my male eye the house is all in readiness several days
before the event—but not to the eye of the ones who are in charge of
final decorations! They say there are "a few little things to do" and
then the house will be ready. I have always been keenly interested in
those "few little things." Decorations in several places; flowers here
and there, accents just right. And when they are all done, they add
up to a quality of unity and beauty in appearance that dresses the
entire house. I find it easier to understand the interior decorator who
says that the big objects in a room are easy; it is the little ones that
come hard because they are what tie the room together.

Some years ago, I had the privilege of sharing in the centennial of
Garrett Biblical Institute—one of the twelve seminaries of the Methodist Church. And as I did, I thought again of the power of small things.

When Garrett Biblical Institute was launched over a hundred years ago in Illinois, it was thrust by God as a bit of leaven into the whole midwest area of the country and church. Almost alone, it assumed the burden of training persons for leadership in our church in this vast area. Soon, not this area only, but the entire church and the world were to feel the powerful influence let loose by this small school. Missionaries, deaconesses, educators, and preachers came from it in increasing numbers until now their total runs into the tens of thousands. Slowly but surely this school has stuck to the job until it has been a primary factor not alone in training men for the ministry but in lifting the educational standards of the entire church.

I met graduates of Garrett wherever I went in Latin America and in the Orient. As missionaries, teachers, and preachers, they were bits of leaven thrust in other bowls of meal.

It was a great and awesome venture of faith on the part of the founders of Garrett to be the ones through whom God thrust that school deep within the kneading trough of a new church in a new society. Yet they did it in complete faith, and that faith has been justified by the fruits of what they did. The process inaugurated then continues today, and it is as sorely needed as ever. What has happened in Garrett Biblical Institute has happened in every institution in the land. It happened in this church when a few courageous people determined that it was to come into existence and backed their faith with their means and their life. Thus the leaven continues to work wherever it is given a chance to work, when men of faith thrust it deep within some area of great need.

III

Surrounded as we are by gigantic events and the tremendous institutions of modern society, each one of us is tempted to throw in the sponge, crying, "What can one man do in all this?" This is not necessarily the cry of a chronic quitter; it is as likely the honest question of an earnest person who wonders whether he can really hope to get something done with his own life.

The answer to the question, "What can one man do?" needs to be phrased carefully: *"Not as much as he wishes but much more than he thinks."* Instances of this abound in every field.

Jane Addams comes to the mind of anyone who has lived in Chicago. She had great dreams for her fabled Hull House. She saw in it a center of human relations that would transform that area of Chicago and perhaps remove the problem of the slum areas. She fought steadily through a long lifetime for the achievement of these and other goals. When she died, they were still dreams. Or were they? Yes, in a sense they were because the slums are still with us, only worse. And crime rates do not indicate a noticeable increase in good-neighbor relations in the neighborhood. But Jane Addams got more done than she saw or could see with her eyes.

You could put it this way: The conscience of the city of Chicago is now alert to the problem which Jane Addams saw, and is supporting her work in a hundred different ways. She blazed a trail and indicated a direction that others have both followed and taken. What did she get done?

Not as much as she wished but more than she thought. How did she do it? By being a bit of good leaven in the vast lump of a great city. By losing her life in it, and by encouraging others to do likewise. It took more time than was given her to see her leaven work its perfect work, but time is on God's side in such matters and men of faith will be content that this is so.

This parable of the leaven helps us understand many great things that have happened in the history of our own country.

In colonial America in the 1770's great confusion and debates raged over what course the colonies should pursue relative to England. They were deep in trouble with the Mother Country on many counts. The Stamp Act had been passed and its enforcement was an open sore of bitterness for all, even for those who tried to remain loyal to England.

What should they do? This was the one question on the minds of all, and no answer was found until Thomas Paine thrust a little book called *Common Sense* deep within the meal of colonial life and thought. Our aim, our purpose, is summed up in a single word, he said. That word is "Freedom." Freedom is our natural right and therefore our lawful objective and purpose. Let all that we do be done in the name of Freedom and let us live under her or die for her.

The leaven spread quickly and soon copies of *Common Sense* were almost as plentiful as Bibles and read at least as eagerly.

Whatever may have been Thomas Paine's other shortcomings, we owe him a debt of gratitude for having the insight and the courage to serve the cause of freedom as he did so long ago.

Now we take freedom for granted—or try to. But as soon as we
turn our gaze away from it, someone tries to steal it or stifle its workings. Freedom continues to be a leaven; it continues to need men
with vision and courage to thrust it deep within the life of a world
addicted to police states, totalitarian regimes, and fear-ridden peoples.
It may seem a small thing at first glance, but it has divine power
with it.

What could one man do to arrest the slow decay in morals throughout England in the eighteenth century? No one knew until John
Wesley inserted himself and his dynamic faith deep within the life of
that country. Then for nearly fifty years that powerful leaven worked.
And when Wesley died, other men were following his example all
over the Western world until a mighty force for the reorganization of
life on spiritual and moral principles had been set in motion. It is
instructive to hear a historian say that the Wesleyan revival saved
England a French Revolution. This and many other things may be
true. The point I want to make now is that Wesley's dream of reviving
the Established Church from within was defeated before his very eyes
and to his greatest sorrow. But his confidence in God was such that
he knew that some other great good would come into being because of
the workings of God through this revival.

Go back a few centuries before Wesley and put the question of
Luther's day: "What can one man do to fight off the infection of the
gospel by the corruption of the church?" Luther's life is the full answer
to what at least one man did do! Not only did he set in motion the
Reformation, but that in turn set in motion a cleansing movement
within the Catholic Church which is called the "Counter-Reformation."

It is hard to stop citing cases of what one man can do when he
inserts himself and his dream or vision in the lump of his day with
the far-reaching results we ourselves see now. But I cannot stop without calling to witness the foremost of all—even Jesus Christ.

IV

What could one man hope to do in the face of things as they were
in the first century? Rome regnant and ruthless; Judaism subjugated
but seething with revolt; religion all but stifled by formalism and
supersition. What could one man do? Let this statement attributed to
Phillips Brooks tell us what one man did do:

ONE SOLITARY LIFE

Here is a man who was born in an obscure village, the child of a peasant woman. He grew up in another obscure village. He worked in a carpenter shop until he was thirty, and then for three years he was an itinerant preacher. He never wrote a book. He never held an office.

He never owned a home. He never set foot inside a big city. He never travelled two hundred miles from the place where he was born. He had no credentials but himself.

He had nothing to do with this world except the naked power of his divine manhood. While still a young man, the tide of popular opinion turned against him. His friends ran away. One of them denied him. He was turned over to his enemies. He went through the mockery of a trial. He was nailed upon a cross between two thieves.

His executioners gambled for the only piece of property he had on earth while he was dying—and that was his coat. When he was dead, he was taken down and laid in a borrowed grave through the pity of a friend.

Nineteen wide centuries have come and gone and today he is the center-piece of the human race and the leader of progress. I am far within the mark when I say that all the armies that ever marched, and all the navies that ever were built, and all the parliaments that ever sat, and all the kings that ever reigned, put together have not affected the life of man upon this earth as powerfully as that one solitary life.

Strange as it may seem to put it this way, each church that bears his name is a part of his continuing effects upon mankind. The leaven of his life and the kingdom of God which he thrust deep within humanity in the first century has, by the grace of God, continued to work toward the realization of that kingdom in the lives of men. The process will continue until his dream is realized and God's will is done on earth even as it is in heaven.

What can one man do? It depends upon several things: the man; the truth of what he wants to do; the completeness with which he loses himself in the achievement of it. Spectators need not apply for honors in this sort of effort. Only those who give themselves—not *of* themselves, but themselves—and all that they have will believe in the power of small things enough to succeed.

V

We in the church need to have another look at the meaning of this parable of the leaven if we are to measure up to the meaning of our discipleship today. Do you ever get the feeling, as I confess I do, that God is trying to thrust us deep within the vast world today in order that we might be His leaven in the whole lump?

Then my cynical streak takes over and tells me that if we are "God's starter," so to speak, in all this, something has gone wrong with it: Either it is dead or it has gone sour and will sour the whole lump. But we cannot give up on the church, can we? If we do, either we give up on everything she stands for or we try to start a new church. There is neither time nor need for that. Forces working for the rejuvenation of the church are readily seen by anyone who will honestly study what is happening in the church today.

Everywhere there is an alert awareness of the utter seriousness of these days.

Everywhere there is a profound conviction that the Christian gospel has a saving word for mankind.

Everywhere there is agreement that that word is "Love." Thomas Paine had the word "Freedom" to thrust into the life of colonial America. We have the word "Love" to thrust within this world of hate, division, and war. And everywhere there is a growing consciousness that that saving word can be spoken only in and through the life of the church.

Everywhere there is acceptance of the simple fact that the church must lose herself in the life of this day if she would speak that word in an effective way. She must be willing to be thrust by God as His leaven deep within the mass of problems and dangers of our time in order to speak His word from within.

Arnold Toynbee has written an unusually optimistic forecast for us. "The twentieth century will be chiefly remembered by future generations not as an era of political conflicts or technical inventions, but as an age in which human society dared to think of the welfare of the whole human race as a practical objective."[1]

Let us hope and pray that this prophecy will prove true; but why, how, and by what marvelous means can society be brought to do it? That is where we come in if we have the courage of our convictions and thrust the word "Love" incarnate in our life deep within the collective life of our day.

I would like to believe that the twentieth century will be remembered as the age in which the members of the Christian churches took seriously our heritage of love and thrust it so deep within the life and thought of all nations and peoples that it brought into being a saving unity, compassion, and community among them. Should this prove to be true, what begins as "the age of the atom" will continue as "the age of love."

3. The Toughest Test Men Face

MATTHEW 7:15-20; 12:33-37; LUKE 6:43-45

I

"Thus you will know them by their fruits" (Matt. 7:20) is as widely used as any other insight of the New Testament. Have you ever wondered why this is so? May it not be because we—all of us—are basically and inescapably pragmatic? Does not life force this on us as a requirement of living? We judge people not by what they say, but by what they do, not by word but by deed; we say, "The proof of the pudding is in the eating." In similar vein we feel a deep permanent truth of the insight, "By their fruits, ye shall know them."

The wide-ranging popularity of this insight must be deserved—and it is! It points up in simple, direct language a universal truth which throws light on a problem all men face.

Before we look at some of the ways which men have used this insight, we ought in fairness to it to grasp the meaning it carried to the writers of the Gospels and to their readers in the early church. This can be put in a word: The parable is a solemn warning to the church to beware of heretics, to be on guard against false prophets who pretended to be genuine.

In a day when we take heresy lightly—even treat it as a term of praise to say, "Oh, I'm a heretic!"—we may find it difficult to appreciate the need for, and the utter seriousness of, this warning to the early church. But try for a moment to see it from where they sat.

The early disciples were a handful of people among the millions in the Mediterranean area. The early church grew rapidly, to be sure, but by the end of the first century when the Gospels were being written and circulated, Christianity was still a small sect, a minority group in every sense of that term. As a minority group, unity was the main source of its strength for survival and hope for the future. Whatever augmented this unity was good; whatever weakened it was evil. All changes in the church were closely studied in the light of their relationship to the unity of the brotherhood.

One of the persistent problems of the church—then and now—was dependable, trustworthy leadership. Journeying evangelists, prophets, and teachers were in continual circulation among the Christian groups, and they frequently sowed the seeds of discord because of radically different teachings. This was particularly true of the prophets, a special class of religious leaders who were supposed to receive private visions and messages from God and therefore were highly respected by laymen and other members of the church. As long as such prophets agreed among themselves in their visions, concord reigned and the unity of the group was unbroken. But when they fell out among themselves, their listeners split and the group began to fall apart.

Consequently, the early Christians were urged to "beware of false prophets who come to you in sheep's clothing but inwardly are ravenous wolves." This is not a warning against all prophets; only false ones. But that posed the real problem. It would be easy enough to beware of false prophets if they were known to be false. Any sensible man would obey this warning gladly if he were sure which prophets were false and which were true.

Like the Hebrews before them in Jeremiah's day, the early church tried to develop ways of testing a prophet to determine whether he was true or false. The efforts of the early Hebrews and the early Christians resulted in essentially the same answer: *The only certain way to test the prophets is "by their fruits."*

Jeremiah said, in effect, "If what a man prophesies actually happens, he is a true prophet. If not, he is false." The early church broadened the base of the test somewhat but kept to the principle that the only way one can actually decide whether a prophet is true or false is to listen to him; then gauge the meaning of what he says for strengthening of the Christian life and the welfare of the Christian group. If he splits the group, or is self-seeking, or refuses to be counseled by the elders of the group, he is a false prophet and should be sent on his way at once.

This parable of the false prophet describes him two ways—neither complimentary—both drawn from the pastoral and rural life of Palestine. One pictures him as a wolf in sheep's clothing; the other as a fig or a grape on a thorn bush (Matt. 7:15-20). One thing binds these two figures of speech together: The heretic is not genuine; he is not interested in the church; he does not belong to the Christian fellowship. As we would say in our own vernacular, "He is a phony"; that is, one who sounds a wrong note all the time.

The Gospel writers were great believers in integrity. They were convinced that one's inner nature would be revealed sooner or later in what one did. Honeyed words and pious postures might deceive for a while, but not for long. The contradiction between the internal and the external man would soon become clear to the discerning observer. Hence we read that "the good man out of his good treasure brings forth good, and the evil man out of his evil treasure brings forth evil; . . . for out of the abundance of the heart the mouth speaks" (Matt. 12:35, 34).

Matthew—always one to sharpen up a phrase until it cuts—says to the Pharisees, "You brood of vipers! How can you speak good, when you are evil?" (Matt. 12:34.) Which is a way of charging that they were evil through and through from the inside out and thus their words were corrupted at their very source.

II

Accepting the teaching of the parable that deeds are the true gauge of the whole man, an interesting question suggests itself: *"If you could be given the pick, what deed or achievement in your life would you like to be remembered by?"* As a matter of hard fact, history seldom consults us about this—sometimes even seems to insult us by it. Shakespeare causes one of his disillusioned agents to cry:

> The evil that men do lives after them;
> The good is oft interred with their bones.[1]

History may not be as arbitrary and unprincipled as all that, but she does make her own choices.

Two of the most forceful and widely heard preachers in America's brief history have been Phillips Brooks and Harry Emerson Fosdick. Both published many books of addresses and sermons. But the very great probability is that both will be remembered for poems that have become deeply beloved hymns of the church. Can you imagine Christ-

mas without singing "O Little Town of Bethlehem"? Phillips Brooks
wrote this poem on his first Christmas eve in Bethlehem as he was
seated on a hill overlooking the city in which our Savior was born. Do
you suppose the church will ever cease loving and using this hymn
which now ranks with "Silent Night" in the affection of all? Phillips
Brooks could hardly ask for a better memorial! It gathers up the finest
fruits of his faith, his dreams, his hopes, and lets us know him by them.

Harry Emerson Fosdick has written many important, scholarly books.
He has been in the thick of every major social engagement of the
church over fifty years. Through his long rich radio ministry, he reached
every corner of the country. Many of us have lighted the candle of
our courage from the flaming torch of his fearless faith. And we have
"favorite Fosdick sermons" that we like to consult and reread.

Notwithstanding all this, Dr. Fosdick himself has said that he will
probably be remembered longest by the hymn: "God of Grace and
God of Glory." If we read it with some knowledge of his life in the
back of our minds, we will see at once that he sings about the qualities
in the life of our Lord that have born their fruit in his own life and
ministry. I may say that Dr. Fosdick impresses me as being quite happy
to be remembered by that hymn. Certainly it comes to the minds of all
of us who know him because, somehow, it fits him and he fits it.
There is a fine integrity between singer and song, between poet and
poem. It is good fruit on a good tree, a good word spoken from a good
heart.

When last I visited Jefferson's home, Monticello, I went to the
humble little graveyard on the mountainside where he and the members of his family are buried. I read again the wish of this great American that he should be chiefly remembered as the author of the provision
for religious freedom in the constitution of Virginia. He will be remembered by this grateful country for many things—all good fruits of
his spirit—and let us hope that his wish shall be granted at least to
the extent that we will include this provision among the many rich
fruits of his life.

III

Which deed or achievement of the Christian Church would you
like to have her known and celebrated for? I have a list of things I
would like to submit, and I do so without hesitation as a full answer

to those critics of the church who would give the impression that she has been a prolific source of evil in life or has been irrelevant to life.

That she has been all too human upon occasion, none can deny, but she can exhibit as rich a harvest of good deeds as any institution known to man—and the end of her contribution is not yet!

I want the church to be known and celebrated not for what she says but for what she does, for the good fruits that she has born in human life.

As a first fruit, she deserves to be known and loved for the way she nurtures us in the worship of God. She alone among human institutions centers her life in this calling. The first and final movement in her life and work is to lead us to the fuller praise of our Creator. She confronts us with *God: God* the Creator, Sustainer, and Redeemer of life; *God* the One in whom we live and move and have our being; *God* the Judge of all the earth; *God* the Father of all mercies to whom erring children may come and find forgiveness for their sins; *God* the One whose love will never let us go.

The church does not create God; she discovers Him and helps others discover Him. She worships Him and leads others in that worship. She seeks to serve Him—and invites all who believe in Him to find their place in His service.

Add to this an equally precious second fruit—her love of Jesus Christ, and her faith that in him we have our clearest insight into God's will for man. Jesus Christ is the center of our life and work today even as he was for the early disciples.

The World Council of Churches is making a momentous discovery. Jesus Christ is the center of the Christian tradition and the many Christian churches are spotted somewhere on the circumference around him, separated from each other and from him. But as we move along our own radius toward the center—toward him—we discover that we are moving ever closer to each other. The closer we draw to him, the nearer we are to each other; the more we center our faith in him, the truer the sense of unity with each other becomes. At Amsterdam, at Evanston, at New Delhi we said with great joy, "Our unity is in Christ," and in saying this we were but giving expression to this experience of finding each other as we seek to confront him. Engaged as the World Council now is in exploring the nature of the unity we seek, we find that we must begin and end with him if we are to know any unity at all.

Nor is the appreciation of this fruit reserved for the World Council of Churches. It is the open secret of why we believe in, love, and are willing to work in the church. The closer we draw to him the more at home we feel in the church, the more willing and abler we are to do the work of the church. I have heard laymen here and elsewhere give it as the reason for what they are doing in the church. Some years ago one of the laymen of our church who was chairman of the Commission on Stewardship and Finance greeted new members with these words, "We want you to love and serve the Lord through this church. That is why we are here and why we welcome you to our fellowship."

It is, therefore, no accident that the symbols of the church center in Jesus Christ. We owe him everything we are and hope to be as a church. In his service, men have gone to the ends of the earth. May we never let the familiarity of that phrase "to the ends of the earth" blind us to the immeasurable amount of sacrifice, hardship, and true glory involved in it! Where Christ leads, men who believe in him must go, not counting the cost or calculating the gain. He is our Lord and our Leader.

I confess to some weariness of spirit when I hear critics of the church say they believe in Christ but not in the church. Were it not for the church—with all her weaknesses—they would know of no Christ to believe in. The disciples who gathered around him in adoration and love were the first church. Their recollections and teachings provided the materials from which the New Testament was written. The continuing church wrote the New Testament, which contains practically all we know of Jesus Christ. The church treasured and taught the New Testament until it became the spiritual discipline of the Christian in all ages. The church has taught this faith, lifted this witness, lived for it, and been willing to die for it; that is why it is available to us today. The love of Christ, the feeling that in him we see God—this is one of the most nourishing fruits of the church.

A third fruit of the church which nourishes all who are willing to be fed by it is the study of the Bible, opening it to all who would know it. The church alone among the institutions of our world is concerned about the Bible—concerned enough to study it and present it to all as a worthy object of study. We call it the Book of Life—as, indeed, it has proved to be. It is the richest deposit of religious experience we have; it contains the only reliable record we have of God's dealings with Israel and the early church and of man's response to Him. In it we find the long ladder of experience up which men climbed to a rich, full belief in God. In it we find the interpretation of man as a child of God, the bearer of an immortal soul, which forever challenges the tyrant and the collectivist who would elevate the group at the expense of the individual. In it we find food for the daily journey and for its continuation beyond the gates of death.

This Bible is a book of comfort, to be sure, but it is much more than that. It is a book of rebuke, of judgment. It is a book of guidance, pointing the way to God for those who have lost Him, giving those who want to serve Him some notion of what it means. While it would be a mistake to treat it as a textbook, we shall want to regard it as a handbook of faith, and study it steadily all our life.

One of the goals of a vital church is the continuous study of this book. It can and ought to become as precious a part of our daily life and thought as ever it was to our most devout forefathers, who in its strength fought off tyrants, crossed oceans, founded colonies, built countries, established missions, and commended it to us as the sun and the summit of wisdom.

A fourth kind of fruit born by the church is the steady effort to bring men into a creative, redemptive fellowship. The fruits I have specified are not to be snatched from the tree of the church and devoured in some solitary corner by self-righteous, hypocritical critics of the church. They are most nourishing when shared in the fellowship of the church. Each one calls upon us to do something in response to them. The worship of God leads to work for God's sake. The discovery of Christ means to follow him now as truly as ever. The study of the Bible is most useful when it is a shared pursuit.

The church seeks to be the fellowship of those who know they are not only "to love God and enjoy Him forever" but must also be willing to bring their own life and the life of their society and world under His judgment. We are members of this fellowship not only to rejoice in the things He has done for our fathers before us, but also to find our way in His holy will as we move into the unknown future. We need the help of each other's experience and insight, the bracing of each other's courage in this. It is our business—if we may call it that— to make *love obvious* wherever we are and in whatever we do.

Nor need we any longer feel as apologetic about this as once we did. A world sadly chastened by its own failures and frightened by the threats of its own power may be willing to listen to the Christian approach to life.

Bertrand Russell has been a kind of gadfly among thinkers in the Western world all his life, and he continues to stir us up one way and another. I have been a student of his writings in all areas where I could understand him, but never thought to live long enough to hear him say what he did in a closing lecture at Columbia University a few years ago. Dealing with *"the cure of war"* he said,

The root of the matter is a very simple and old-fashioned thing, a thing so simple that I am almost ashamed to mention it, for fear of the derisive smile with which wise cynics will greet my words. The thing I mean— please forgive me for mentioning it—is love, Christian love, or compassion. If you feel this, you have a motive for existence, a guide for action, a reason for courage, an imperative necessity for intellectual honesty.[2]

I suggest that the church is as essential to Christian love as Christian love is to the church. I know of no way of saying which comes first, but I am certain they are inseparable.

IV

If we were given the right to indicate the one thing we would like to have Christ Church Methodist, New York City, known for, what would it be? I am sure many answers would leap to the minds of all of us, and they might be quite different largely because of our differing experiences in the life of the church.

If it were given to me to lift up the one fact by which I should like to have the Christian Church known, I would lay hands on one that is as yet imperfectly realized. By that I mean it is partly true and partly not. Some of us see it, believe it, and are willing to live by it. Others either do not see it or see it only fitfully or are not willing to let it become a part of their experience in the church.

This is what I am talking about: *I would like to have us known as the church which has the courage of its convictions;* The courage to believe in the kingdom of God; the courage to plan for its service; the courage to share gladly of our time, talents, and goods in its life and work. This is no new dream, nor is it the peculiar property of any one church. It ought to be true of all. At least, it is my most precious dream for every church I have ever served or will ever serve.

It is not unusual for a church to have convictions, that is, to know what the Christian's central convictions are. Nor is it exceptional for a church to study and discuss their meaning for life today. But it is unusual for a church to be guided by them in the formulation of its life and policy. All too frequently the church is a creature of society— and is content to be so. It ceases to be a creative, forceful, implacable critic of society and is content to lift occasional demurrers; but neither man nor society can be helped much, let alone have the path of salvation pointed out by occasional admonitions. The prophets of Israel, the Apostles, and the Reformers have shown us the better way—but few of us have the courage to walk in it.

And when the church does screw up her courage to the point of real usefulness, some of us grow nervous and uneasy, and counsel caution or cut our pledge, hoping thereby to cripple the church because it does not do what we think it should do. I would like to have Christ Church Methodist known far and wide as a fellowship in which there is genuine friendliness, an honest meeting of minds even where there is difference of opinion, the courage to face the great issues of our day in the light of our deepest Christian convictions.

The fruits of that kind of church will be good because they will come from a good heart: a heart in which love of God and love of man hold sway. "Thus you will know them by their fruits."

4. Oh, We Mean Well!

I

Jesus was sudden death on well-wishers, that is, people who wanted to settle for good intentions. Time and again he laid it on the line for them: "Not everyone who says . . . Lord, Lord . . . but he who does the will of my Father" (Matt. 7:21); "No one who puts his hand to the plow and looks back is fit for the kingdom of God" (Luke 9:62). Finally, almost in desperation, he confronts the multitude as well as the disciples with a series of short parables that try to drive home the single point that good intentions are not enough for discipleship.

While we need to restudy and relearn all of Jesus' teachings, this one seems especially urgent for the Christian Church these days.

As Luke reconstructs events, Jesus and his disciples were journeying toward Jerusalem. This was to be their final and fateful journey together to the big city. Jerusalem drew him as a magnet draws iron filings. He knew the Holy City to be the stronghold of Roman cruelty and power, the citadel of Jewish authority, the shrine of ancestral faith—where certain misunderstanding and possible tragedy awaited him and all who were associated with him. He knew that once he was there a showdown with religious and civil authorities was all but inevitable, and he had dark premonitions as to the outcome.

As we get the picture, Jesus had two types of followers as he journeyed toward Jerusalem. Far and away the larger number was "the multitude" who halfway believed him to be the Messiah and wanted to be on hand for the grand opening of the kingdom he was bringing. It was, according to tradition, to be a day of glory and triumph—with rewards and rejoicing for all.

Jesus' disciples constituted the rest of his companions. By disciples we should probably understand not alone the Twelve, but many more who followed him faithfully. These seemed only dimly to perceive that this was no ordinary trek to the Holy City: This was it!—the long awaited day when God through His Son was to announce, inaugurate, and unveil to all His kingdom.

Understandably Jesus wanted to know whom he could depend upon in the dire days ahead. He saw the excited multitudes who were following him, drawn by the rumor he was about to start the long-awaited kingdom of God. They wanted to be in on that—who wouldn't! They wanted to be there when the old order passed and the new one began. Obviously they needed some stern words of warning.

The disciples were not much better. He had surprised them discussing the order of their importance in the kingdom. Clearly, they intended to bask in the glory of the great days ahead.

Of course he had tried to bring both multitude and disciples down to earth before, but without much success. It must have been as frustrating to him as to any teacher to know that he was saying one thing while they were hearing another. But, frustrating or no, he called a halt to the journey long enough to have another try at confronting them with the stark realities beckoning him and all who followed him to Jerusalem.

He wanted to be sure they understood the seriousness of what they were doing. He wanted people generally and his disciples particularly to appreciate the revolutionary nature of the kingdom he was inaugurating. He wanted them to glimpse the hard personal price each one might be called on to pay for it, for he was certain that dark days lay ahead.

Turning to the multitude, he said,

If any one comes to me and does not hate his own father and mother and wife and children and brothers and sisters, yes, and even his own life, he cannot be my disciple. Whoever does not bear his own cross and come after me, cannot be my disciple. For which of you, desiring to build a tower, does not first sit down and count the cost, whether he has enough to complete it? Otherwise, when he has laid a foundation, and is not able to finish, all who see it begin to mock him, saying, This man began to build, and was not able to finish. Or what king, going to encounter another king in war, will not sit down first and take counsel whether he is able with ten thousand to meet him who comes against him with twenty thousand. And if not, while the other is yet a great way off, he sends an embassy and asks terms of peace. So therefore, whoever of you does not renounce all that he has cannot be my disciple (Luke 14:26:33).

II

With good cause, one New Testament scholar gives these parables the title: "Warnings against precipitancy and half-heartedness in following Christ."[1] Jesus makes four points in his brief discourse—and they are as relevant to discipleship today as ever they were.

First, a choice is required and a cross must be borne. We continue to be shocked by his firm demand, "If any one comes to me and does not hate his own father and mother and wife and children and brothers and sisters, yes, and even his own life, he cannot be my disciple." "Hate" is a strong word, and as used here it simply does not mean what we usually mean by it. It means choice against these relationships, choice to leave them and follow him no matter what the cost. Jesus knew how hard it was to do that—because he had done it. But he knew it had to be done. The only man who could hope to survive the fearful days ahead was one who had staked his all on it. Such a choice is bound to be a heavy cross, but it must be daily assumed by all who would follow him and be loyal to him to the end. A choice is required and a cross must be borne.

A second warning is couched in the parables of counting the cost of building a temple before you ever start and the wisdom of a king who evaluates his strength before he gets in a war. This is a surprisingly modern bit of advice. Jesus is saying, in effect, count the cost of following me, count it with great care. Be sure you have enough faith and strength to see it clear through no matter how hard it will be before you start. If you doubt whether you have what it takes, don't go any further; turn away; go home—go anywhere but with me to Jerusalem.

A third emphasis warns them to renounce all possessions as well as all earthly relationships: "So therefore, whoever of you does not renounce all that he has cannot be my disciple." Jesus knew how hard it was to love God and Mammon, so hard that it could not be done. He did not try it himself and he warned his disciples to make as clean a break as possible with any entangling alliances with the world. It is as hard as ever for a man who is deeply concerned about his property

OH, WE MEAN WELL!

to be deeply concerned about his soul. Even though Christians have not fulfilled this demand in any outstanding way, its radical nature is forever before us as something we must do. The Emperor Julian, who turned Christian and then reverted to paganism, launching persecutions against the churches, once said, in sarcasm, "In order that they may enter more easily into the kingdom of heaven in the way in which their wonderful law bids them, I have ordered all the money of the church of Edessa to be seized."

Francis of Assisi became St. Francis because of Jesus' word, "Whoever of you does not renounce all that he has cannot be my disciple." Freed then from the desire to get, to keep, to own, to enjoy possessions, Francis turned toward God and His world with an openness of heart and love seldom equaled and never surpassed.

A final warning to the well-wishers and would-be disciples is to keep their convictions strong and creative, not to lose their enthusiasm for the kingdom, nor let their loyalty to it run down. He urged those who wanted to follow him to do so with the full awareness of what they were doing—then they would be like salt that was really salty. But if their convictions faltered, if their loyalty waned, if their enthusiasm petered out, then they would be quite worthless. It is clear that, in Jesus' book, there are no "nominal Christians." He would not accept our easygoing distinction between active and nominal Christians. I'm afraid he would insist upon his own distinction: *Disciple or not*. That, I submit, continues to be a rough distinction.

These parables are indeed a warning "against precipitancy and half-heartedness in following Christ." Good intentions and well-wishing have their proper place, but they are not enough for any of the serious work of Christian discipleship then or now.

III

There are halls of fame for people who excel in many things. If there were one for those who excel in good intentions, who of us could escape serious consideration for it? But we are not disposed to joke about it, are we? Nor doubt the truth of the adage, "The road to Hell is paved with good intentions"—I'm tempted to add "of Christians." For we know that, of themselves, good intentions are not enough.

In fact, the longest, costliest step in the process of spiritual maturity is from dream to deed, from insight to action, from conviction to life.

But it must be taken else the dream, the insight, and the conviction will waste away and finally perish. That is why Christian ethics maintains a delicate balance between motive and deed, intention and action. It never permits us to think that when we have drawn a blueprint we have built a building. Any layman in architecture knows the value of a blueprint, knows how essential it is to a building. But a building is much more than a blueprint. Christian ethics tries to keep this balance between dream and deed, between intention and action. For if ever we lose that balance the scales tip either toward the visionary who has no sense of fact or toward the realist who has no vision. It is hard to say which of these is more to be pitied.

The true disciple of Jesus Christ tries to maintain this balance because he knows that good intentions are not enough for the work of building the kingdom.

The best of intentions is not enough for either *the great commandment or the great commission* of our Lord.

The great commandment, he said, is to love God and man utterly. This, obviously, goes far beyond anything that would qualify as "good intentions." This means decision, commitment, consecration—or it means nothing at all.

It is not presumptious to try to say what the great commandment means, though it would surely be presumptious were we to give the impression that any one of us can know all that it does mean. Clearly, though, to love God means several things—and all push far beyond good intentions.

To love God is to know Him as our Creator, to own Him as our Father. It is to be always sensitive to His presence in His world, to be aware of Him and to rejoice in Him. It is to thrill to His presence in the unfolded and unfolding world in which we live. It is to be driven to our knees "when I consider thy heavens, the work of thy fingers, the moon and the stars which thou hast ordained," there to ask in hushed wonder, "What is man that thou art mindful of him? And the son of man that thou visitest him?" It is to find in him the daily personal companion of our spirits whose very presence brings us the peace, joy, and sense of purpose we need. It is to seek our way in His will in complete confidence that as we find and follow it we shall be led not only "beside the still waters" but out on storm-tossed seas where men must seek ports of justice, brotherhood, and peace guided only by occasional glimpses of His stars. To love Him means to find the strength and purpose of our life in Him, to worship Him with all our soul, and to follow where He leads with all the energies of our life.

To love man utterly runs as far beyond good intentions as does the love of God. It means to own all men as fellow creatures of God, made in His image even as we are. It is to learn to look at other people with trust and understanding, and, as they fail, with compassion and forgiveness. It is to refuse to be blocked away from anyone by hate, prejudice, or fear and to try by every means at our disposal to build a creative relationship with him.

All this runs as far beyond good intentions as the Declaration of Independence ran beyond the desire for freedom in the hearts of the American colonists. Oh, the desire was there both uttered and unexpressed for decades, but it was without form and largely void of content until the ones who cherished it moved out into the area of public commitment and action, saying, "This is what we believe, this is what we propose to do about it, and for the achievement of it, we pledge 'our lives, our fortunes, and our sacred honor.' "

You may have heard of the British missionary in India who was preaching the love of God and man among the untouchables. When he had finished his discourse an elderly man asked, "Do you really love us as you say your Christ bids you do?" The missionary answered, "Yes." Lifting a sorry-looking arm, the old man said, "Then wash my sores."

Or as Jesus would have said, "You do not love your brother so long as you pass by on the other side. You love him only when you stop, bind up his wounds, take him to an inn and make provision for his care."

Love of man is not the syrupy sentimentalism it sometimes seems. It means entering into the arena of public action and commitment in behalf of causes in which we believe and of persons whose rights are endangered. We are finding this out as we seek to remove the stain of segregation from every part of our church thought and life. It cannot be done speedily. It cannot be done easily. But it can and must and will be done when we realize that good intentions are not enough, and move firmly and fairly beyond them into the realm of church law, church policy and program, and fellowship within the local church.

If timid souls think this agitation, then let them rest assured that that is exactly what it is intended to be. An agitator is basically someone who stirs people up until they are ready to move beyond intentions into action. Agitators, though they have a bad name now, are of good as well as bad varieties. Their good or evil depends upon the cause they serve, not necessarily upon their own mode of furthering it. We need to remember that the charge was made of the early Christians that "they upset the world." I would think that that required a fair amount of agitation! Justice William O. Douglas describes William Lloyd Garrison, a violent and dramatic Abolitionist in pre-Civil War days, as "more roundly cursed than anyone in American life." Yet Garrison knew exactly what he was doing all the time. In the 1830's he said, "Slavery will not be overthrown without excitement, a most tremendous excitement." Without subscribing to all he said, I should like to subscribe to the essential wisdom of his insight into one fundamental of effective social action: a tremendous excitement deep within the souls of people that will lead them to say, "This thing must go!"

I think we would agree that the Christian Church is all but weighed down with good intentions toward all men—intentions born of our nurture in the Christian heritage. But aren't you shocked by the extreme difficulty of getting effective crusades to implement these intentions off the ground? Each time we try to launch an all-out drive against the continued manufacture and testing of nuclear weapons, for example, we are all but swept away by counsels of caution, prudence, and worldly wisdom which set at nought divinely inspired insights. We churchmen need to take to heart something Joe Louis said as he listened to a sports reporter tell him exactly how he ought to fight Billy Conn. "You talk a good fight," said Joe, who had to get into the ring the next day.

To love man is to take his problems as our problems, to lose ourselves in them with understanding and compassion, and to share as much as we are able in the effort to solve them.

IV

Good intentions are not enough to carry out the great commission of our Lord, to go to the ends of the earth with the gospel. Paul and every missionary since his day have found this to be true. David Livingstone, one of the most virile Christian leaders of all time, had as his motto, "Fear God, and work hard." He learned it in his austere home in Scotland and practiced it all his life. As a matter of fact his biography seems to be crowded with events that shook the foundations of Africa and of the outside world's relationship with Africa. One biographer gives us this thumbnail sketch of him:

> Within the field of vision we see moving the solitary figure of a white man with peaked cap, whose keen observant eyes note every detail about him, who speaks gently to all and reads much in a Book ready to his hand. We see him remonstrating patiently and courteously with hostile natives and slave-traders; contending against stupidity and treachery, against hunger and weakness and pain, perpetually baffled and disappointed but always daunt-less and hopeful and calm. We see him pressing ever forward, indomitable in his determination to bring about the redemption of the people and the land.
>
> We see him grow old in his sacrificial service, grey and toothless, and racked with fever and excruciating pain, walking with ulcered feet and swimming brain—but always forward.
>
> We see him stricken, his strength slowly ebbing under his privations and hardships, lying in a hut in the bush, his thoughts outreaching the worn and disabled frame and travelling onwards on his quest.
>
> Dimly in the darkness and loneliness of the tropical night we see him on his knees, his tired body at last at rest, but his spirit winging its way on further adventurous flight.
>
> The vision fades but the story remains, a continuous inspiration in its revelation of the power and dignity and possibilities of the human soul.[2]

Livingstone belongs to that select company of souls who not only know that good intentions are not enough, but know also that their most strenuous efforts will not complete the really big jobs. Even so, they tackle them with all the energy they have and for all of the days God gives them to live. Then they hand them over to others, confident both in what they have done and in the fact that the work will continue. All great men of action are men of great faith in God, in themselves, and in what He will yet bring to pass.

For forty years George Norris was a figure to be reckoned with in the political and social thought of America. That was the length of time he served Nebraska as Representative and Senator in Washington. And, from first to last, he fought what he called the efforts of "special interests" to control our way of life. At the end of his career of public service, the old man told a younger colleague, "I have fought the good fight with all that was in me. Now there is no strength left.

Other hands must take up the burdens. Remember, the battle against injustice is never won!"

Like any other religious leader, Paul was led by great dreams and powerful insights, but he was not content to contemplate them, nor was he exhausted by them. When summing up his life effort for a young preacher called Timothy, he did not say, "I have had a great vision; I have had a wonderful dream." Not Paul! He said, "I have fought a good fight, I have finished my course, I have kept the faith." And there we have it: the life work of Paul—a positive, declarative statement of faith born of a positive, declarative life of Christian discipleship. That is the way Paul summed up his Christian witness. How would we sum up ours?

5. Persistence Is a Virtue

I

Sometimes I think we can see and hear ourselves each time one of the disciples of our Lord says something. The disciples were so human! Small wonder we feel at home with them and can understand their anxieties, their doubts, their flaming hopes, and their quiet despair. We can also appreciate their confusion about the meaning and the practice of prayer. Like good Jews, they probably prayed daily—but it had become more a routine habit than a spring of living waters bringing peace, power, and joy to them. Yet they were keenly aware of how much prayer meant to Jesus and how much less it had come to mean to them. Prayer was the most vital and vitalizing part of his day. The tireder he was, the longer he prayed. The more difficult the day's work, the more certainly he sought out a place where he could commune with his Father in an intense, personal way unheard by man.

The relationship between his prayers and his life was not lost on his disciples. That is why, on a certain day when they were journeying to Jerusalem, they waited until he had finished his period of prayer; then, one bolder than the rest—perhaps needier than the rest—said, "Lord, teach us to pray." This he did—both with a pattern of prayer and a parable stressing the need of persistence in prayer. He said to them in effect, "Here is a form of prayer, but it will mean little to you unless you persist in it. Do not separate the prayer from persistence in praying."

Then with this parable he underscored the need for persistence:

Once, in a certain place, Jesus was at prayer. When he ceased, one of his disciples said, Lord, teach us to pray, as John taught his disciples. He answered, When you pray, say,

Father, thy name be hallowed;
Thy kingdom come.
Give us each day our daily bread.
And forgive us our sins,
For we too forgive all who have done us wrong.
And do not bring us to the test.

He added, Suppose one of you has a friend who comes to him in the middle of the night and says, My friend, lend me three loaves, for a friend of mine on a journey has turned up at my house, and I have nothing to offer him; and he replies from inside, Do not bother me. The door is shut for the night; my children and I have gone to bed; and I cannot get up and give you what you want. I tell you that even if he will not provide for him out of friendship, the very shamelessness of the request will make him get up and give him all he needs. And so I say unto you, ask, and you will receive; seek, and you will find; knock, and the door will be opened. For everyone who asks receives, he who seeks finds, and to him who knocks, the door will be opened.

Is there a father among you who will offer his son a snake when he asks for fish, or a scorpion when he asks for an egg? If you, then, bad as you are, know how to give your children what is good for them, how much more will the heavenly Father give the Holy Spirit to those who ask him!" (Luke 11:1-13, NEB.)

II

Here is one parable that must have leaped straight out of the experiences our Lord. Then, as now, unexpected guests bring unanticipated crises in the home and the kitchen. And should guests come at night, the crisis is certain to be more widespread and much more acute. For room must be found for rest—which meant shifting of sleeping children in the small and usually overcrowded houses of Palestine; food must be provided for refreshment, which might mean a quick trip to the neighbors for bread or something else. If the neighbor and his family are asleep, too bad, but no matter, he must be roused by continuous knocking. Even if he tells the caller to keep quiet and go away, he must persist. Again and again and again he must knock until the neighbor is thoroughly awake and finally overwhelmed by his persistence. Then he will get up, give him bread, and perhaps some friendly, heartfelt advice on one or two related matters!

Now, said Jesus, with a twinkle in his eye, if persistence is the clue to success here and elsewhere, surely it will help in prayer. The man who needs bread has a right to persist in search of it until he gets it. We who need things much more important than bread must be ready to persist in our search for them until we get them. So he makes a simple and penetrating point in this parable: The earnestness we praise elsewhere in life is essential to creative prayer.

I doubt whether his disciples needed to learn that lesson any more than we do today. We find it easy enough to praise persistence as a value elsewhere in life but are reluctant to practice it in our religion. Yet, if experience is any monitor at all, it is essential to our religious life and especially to our prayer life. If we want our prayer life to be rich, creative, and refreshing, if we want our participation in the life and work of the church to be strong and vibrant with hope and conviction, then we will want to give this matter of persistence renewed consideration.

III

The need for persistence is widely acknowledged in all creative endeavors from kindergarten to the research laboratory, from athletics to art.

Every teacher and parent knows that the real secret in the learning process is concern, interest, a determination to know. We say the child must be "motivated," he must be interested in what he is doing or he will go about it with all the zest of a quarry slave being flogged to work. There can be no creative learning without the kind of interest and concern which makes the child persist until he actually succeeds. We who have seen our children go through school realize how indebted we are to teachers who can awaken and encourage the kind of interest that causes them to keep themselves at the job until it is well done. This kind of creative persistence is born from within though it can be nurtured from without. The wise persistence of parent and teacher can combine to encourage interest and tenacity in the child, but until that is done, his education is a lost cause. The best teachers may not be the ones who know the most about the subject—though that never hurts good teaching—they are the ones who make us want to know more and stimulate us to find out more on our own.

Every athlete appreciates the need for persistence if he is to excel in his sport. Scarcely a week passes now without some story of how a skater or swimmer or ball player has literally slaved at his chosen task until he has mastered it. His whole life is organized around the undertaking: food, rest, play, sleep—he knows that everything must fit into the pattern of successful discipline, and he persists in it until it is done. That is both the making and the meaning of being a champion.

If you have read a biography of Thomas A. Edison you will recall the phenomenal persistence with which he worked at every problem he faced. Each one was a vital personal challenge to him—a challenge he must meet, and could meet only by complete concentration on it. I think I shall never forget the patient persistence with which he and his assistants searched for the right material to use as a filament in the new electric light. For months they had trembled on the verge of success only to be disappointed in one material after another. Everything they could think of they tried—until, finally, they discovered what they had been looking for so steadily.

It is not necessary to multiply illustrations of the meaning of persistence to success in life. Yet I cannot refrain from sharing an experience I had with Oren Skinner of the Connick Studios of Boston who was asked to design, execute, and install a lovely colored window in a chapel in the Mount Vernon Place Methodist Church in Baltimore, Maryland.

When we in the church determined we wanted the window I went to Boston to talk with the ones in charge of the Connick Studios. Oren Skinner listened carefully to my outline of our hopes and dreams for the church, the chapel, and the window. Then his interest seemed to take on a deeper hue as he began to let it sink in and make it his. Suddenly he suggested that I come back later in the day and we would talk further.

This I did and was surprised to have him hand me a rough sketch or two that he had worked out in the meantime. They meant very little to me because they were for the professional in art rather than for the amateur. However, he said, "My colleagues and I would like to work along these lines for awhile. If we come up with something significant, I will call you."

Weeks and months passed and the call never came—but finally Mr. Skinner came in person bringing a watercolor sketch that commanded the immediate interest of all of us in the church. He asked to be shown where we planned to place the window, and spent several hours there.

He measured the light in the morning, the afternoon, and the early evening. Then he seemed to recede within himself once more, and finally said, "We are not wholly satisfied with our sketch." And back he went to Boston. More time passed before he returned with another sketch, which not only pleased them but pleased us in the church.

Wanting a certain shade of blue he and his associates worked through dozens of different efforts until they had it. And so it went until the window was finished. A workman accompanied it from Boston to Baltimore and hovered over it like a mother hovering over her baby. On the day it was unveiled, Oren Skinner and the man who had installed it saw the light come flooding through, illuminating the symbols in the window, lighting the chapel with meanings that will live forever: then they looked toward each other, smiled a bit, nodded, and said to us, "Will it do?"

Talk about persistence! Talk about the patient nurture of the creative insight until it becomes incarnate in a work of art that will live forever—there you have it!

IV

The need for persistence in religion was no new theme in Jewish thought when Jesus raised it with his disciples in this parable. In fact, the high points in their heritage were so many peaks of persistence.

When God wanted to purge the children of Israel of their sins before admitting them to the Promised Land, He had them spend forty years in the wilderness. Generation after generation came and passed away before the Promised Land was safely theirs. When sin struck them blind once more, the Exile came bringing the destruction of Jerusalem and the Temple, and life in a foreign country for most of them. Faith was hard, but they were equal to the test—they persevered in faith until 150 years later their children's children went back to try it again in the homeland.

Rabbi Solomon Freehof has given the great prophets the wonderful title "stormers of heaven." Certainly they were marvels of faithful persistence. For forty years Isaiah responded faithfully to the voice of the Lord. Hosea, Jeremiah, and Ezekiel were equally faithful over long periods of time even though things were going from bad to worse in the life of their people.

Through it all, Israel learned something about the patience and persistence of God. When God wants something done, He sticks to it until it is done. When He wants something said, He "raises up a prophet." When He wants a people purified of sin, He causes a wilderness or an exile to come. He who is so persistent, whose will never falters, requires of His people loyalty, faithful persistence, no matter where He leads them. And time seems to be on His side. Small wonder the psalmist cried out that a thousand years in His sight were but as yesterday when it was passed and as a watch in the night.

When Jesus recommended persistence to his disciples as an essential of faith he was standing on hardwon ground, ground he had tested himself, and was to test again in Gethsemene and on Calvary. He could look back on his own long wrestle with temptation in the wilderness; he had had many an all-night vigil in prayer; he had fled the crowds repeatedly in order to find the time to keep in close communion with his Father. His entire life and ministry were dependent now on the sustaining power and presence of God. It was more important to him to be right with God than with man; more important to be close to God than to man; more important to be loyal to God than to man. Prayer for him was not idle piety, no casual afterthought. It was purpose, strength, and life—and it required the best that he had and all that he had. It was a turning of his whole life toward God: his fears and hopes, his dreams and plans. That is why he did not believe for one moment that prayer was a form of magic. It was his deepest, most determined, most completely conscious effort to break through all barriers and keep in close personal touch with God.

The more we know about the psychology and physiology of our own makeup, the better we appreciate the wisdom of his insistence on persistence. Only as we apply ourselves earnestly to something are we wholly alive to it. It is amazing how many things we do "half consciously," as we say. And that is about the way we do it, too: half conscious, half awake, half alive, half aware. There may be some things we can do that way: walk when we are half asleep and pick up and put down our feet automatically. When we are dead tired, we only half hear what someone may be saying to us. When we are unable to concentrate our attention on a problem, it eludes us continually.

Said Jesus, If you are ever going to learn how to pray, you must concentrate on it, be deeply alive to it, concerned about it, aware of its enormous importance, and you must stick to it until you get an answer.

Jesus was certain that God heard and answered prayer—not the way he wanted it answered always, but God gave His own answer and Jesus was willing to accept it.

The discipline by which he learned to listen to God gave way to the discipline by which he was able to follow where God led. "No one ever gave such assurance to prayer as Jesus," says one scholar.[1] True enough—but no one ever handled prayer with more firmness and greater appreciation of the right and wrong ways to use it—and the need for persistence in it.

True prayer is always an exploration in the vastness of the will of God in search of meanings by which to live and a personal companion with whom to live. If it took persistence for Columbus to discover a new world, how much more persistence ought it take to explore the meaning of the will of God for man. There is a cumulative intensity in Jesus' word: You must ask, you must seek, you must knock with increasing earnestness—and keep at it until you get an answer!

How all this rebukes the way we think about prayer and what we usually call praying! Where in the tenative, half-dubious efforts of a few fugitive moments in which we either whisper a few words learned in childhood or none at all, where, I ask you, in all this is there anything comparable to the earnest, determined, tenacious, persistent wrestling with God in prayer which we see in Christ and hear him commend to his disciples?

John Knox was closer to the heart of prayer when he used it as a way of winning Scotland. As a matter of fact he was interrupted by his wife in the midst of a midnight prayer in behalf of his beloved land. She pleaded with him to seek rest from "the terrible agony of intercession." Knox rebuked her with the reply that through his prayer he had already won half of Scotland, and that if she had not broken in upon him, he would have won all of it by daybreak.

V

Jesus would have had a very firm answer, I think, to our usual complaints about prayer.

To us who say or think, "I don't pray because I don't believe in it," he would answer, "Then you don't believe in God. For if you did, you would both believe in prayer and would pray."

To the objection, "I just can't believe that God hears and answers prayer," he would answer, "God must be no more than a word to you. He cannot be a fact you must live with or you would take Him with utmost seriousness. The God who created you a being who can hear, know, and love must be able to do at least as well as His creatures. Why do you think He cannot hear and answer your prayers when the cumulative experiences of men point to the opposite conclusion?"

To us who say, "Well, I've tried it and I get nothing out of it," he would say, "How hard, how insistently and how wholeheartedly have you really tried to reach God through prayer? Why did you quit trying? Did you quit believing in God—was that why you quit trying to pray to Him? Remember, you must put everything you have into it or you will get nothing, absolutely nothing out of it."

Or, as one interpreter has put it, this parable illustrates "the indifference of God to anything less than the best there is in man—the determination of Heaven not to hear what we are not determined that Heaven shall hear."[2]

To us who say, "Well, I have tried prayer and it doesn't do any good; it doesn't help a bit. I didn't get what I wanted and I got what I tried to avoid," he would answer, "I did not get what I first wanted either, though I asked for it, but I did get what I most wanted: a knowledge of God's will and the strength to follow it. What more do you want? What more can you ask than that? But don't ask it unless you really mean it. Assuming you are sincere about it, then ask it with all your soul and keep on asking until you get it."

That is a lesson worth learning. He is a leader worth following.

6. Our Day of Judgment

I

My first intimation that there might be a Day of Judgment came not from the Bible but from an aged veteran of the Civil War, who was a neighbor in boyhood days. The old man spent all his time, apparently, on the books of Daniel and Revelation. He was filled to overflowing with their dire predictions of the end of the world; he confidently awaited the Second Coming of our Lord. Each morning he would come out of the house, look up at the sky, and say almost joyfully, "This could be Judgment Day." When asked what would happen if it were, he exclaimed, "The saints will be caught up in glory and the rest will be thrown into a sea of fire." That was an arresting thought, especially to a small boy. But we knew our neighbor pretty well and paid little attention to it, though we did take some delight in threatening one another with that sea of fire upon occasion!

Even those of us who have edged away from anything like belief in a Day of Judgment will want to face the fact that we find it in some form throughout the Bible. There is no way we can edit the notion of divine judgment out of either the Bible or life itself. We find it or something like it in both places. And I suspect we find it in the Bible because it is to be found throughout life. We are awakened to the full meaning of its importance for life by biblical insights into it even as a discovery of it in life reawakens our awareness of the biblical descriptions of it.

The conviction that God is the Judge before whom man and nations must and do stand in judgment has to be accepted as an essential part of the biblical notion of life and our belief that we live in a moral world. Certainly it is implicit in the conviction that God created the world,

45

called it good, set before man the choice of good and evil, and made it clear that his life depended upon that choice.

The legends of creation and the history of Israel resound with the ominous note of divine judgment. Adam and Eve were cast out of Eden because of their disobedience. Cain was set adrift on the face of the earth through disobedience. For two hundred years the prophets of Israel warned that her disobedience would surely bring judgment, punishment, and disaster. Amos spoke of the Day of the Lord that was to be a day of darkness and not light, during which the punishment of Israel's sins would fall upon all—and none could escape or survive. When Ezekiel heard the sad news of the destruction of Jerusalem, the Temple, and the royal family, he accepted it as the inevitable fruit of disobedience to the will of God: the judgment of the Lord had fallen upon those who deserved it.

Isaiah opened his prophecy with a lament over his people who had fallen under the judgment of God because they had called "evil good and good evil" (5:20). He warned his people to

> Wash yourselves; make yourselves clean, . . .
> cease to do evil,
>   learn to do good;
> seek justice
>   correct oppression (Isa. 1:16-17)

But it remained for the little-known prophet of Malachi, who lived three hundred years after Isaiah, to give us our most vivid description of what he thought the Day of Judgment would be like. After listing Israel's many sins, he says, "For behold, the day comes, burning like an oven, when all the arrogant and all evildoers will be stubble; the day that comes shall burn them up, says the Lord of hosts, so that it will leave them neither root or branch" (Mal. 4:1).

Book after book in the Bible—and some not included in the canon—sound a similar note: There will be a Day of Judgment—a day of darkness, a day of chaos, a day of fear and flight, a day of starvation and agony, a day of fire. So characteristic is this emphasis that we are forced in all honesty to say that the somber note of judgment—the judgment of God—is an essential part of the Bible and biblical thought on life and history.

So, instead of soft-pedaling it, or trying to edge away from it uneasily,

I suggest that we address ourselves to it directly.

Let us (1) chart as carefully as we can its actual growth in the Bible; (2) study the parable of the Last Judgment; and (3) inquire into its contemporary meanings.

II

In his careful study of Judaism,[1] George Foot Moore calls attention to two characteristics of the idea of divine judgment in the Bible: (1) it runs throughout Hebrew thought; (2) the meaning of the idea itself underwent a profound change over the centuries.

Initially, the idea of divine judgment was associated with the punishment that came on those who disobeyed God. It was a Day of Judgment for Adam and Eve when they were discovered in disobedience by God and expelled from Eden. It was a Day of Judgment for Cain when he failed to justify his ways before God and was sent out to roam the earth. As we have seen, the prophets regarded historical events like the destruction of the city, the Temple, the execution of a king, and the deportation of peoples into exile as days of judgment.

George Foot Moore calls attention to these facts and says that at first, "historical crises which determined the fate of nations (were) religiously interpreted as judgments in fact"—judgments of God pronounced at definite times and places in history. Later, and for a variety of reasons, the notion of divine judgment ". . . was transformed in imagination into a great assize at the end of the present epoch of history, with God sitting on His judgment throne pronouncing doom upon rulers and nations."[2] Daniel gives us a vivid picture of this development:

As I looked,
thrones were placed
and one that was ancient of days took his seat;
his raiment was white as snow,
and the hair of his head like pure wool;
his throne was fiery flames,
its wheels were burning fire.
A stream of fire issued
and came forth from before him;
a thousand thousands served him,
and ten thousand times ten thousand stood before him;
the court sat in judgment,
and the books were opened.

I looked then because of the sound of the great words which the horn was speaking. And as I looked, the best was slain, and its body destroyed and given over to be burned with fire. As for the rest of the beasts, their dominion was taken away, but their lives were prolonged for a season and a time. I saw in the night visions,

> and behold, with the clouds of heaven
>   there came one like a son of man,
> and he came to the Ancient of Days
>   and was presented before him.
> And to him was given dominion and glory and kingdom,
> that all peoples, nations, and languages
>   should serve him;
> his dominion is an everlasting dominion,
>   which shall not pass away,
> and his kingdom one
>   that shall not be destroyed.

Daniel 7:9-14

In Enoch, a noncanonical book which influenced early Christians almost as much as any other, we discover a notion of the Day of Judgment that is startling, to say the least. No longer is it something that occurs to men in history. It is actually the Last Day—the day when the whole of creation moves into a new phase of meaning. The fallen angels, the unfaithful shepherds, the blind sheep of Israel, all are brought before the throne of God set up in Palestine. There they are tried, convicted, and cast into an abyss of fire. Then the golden age on earth and in heaven begins under the reign of God's annointed Messiah.

The idea of a Day of Judgment runs throughout the Dead Sea Scrolls that we have been hearing so much about over the last decade. For the community whose life is reflected in these Scrolls were confidently expecting an epoch of conflict in which the evil forces of the world would be totally defeated in a series of great battles, and the forces of righteousness, under the guidance of a divine Person, would reign supreme. Then would occur a great Day of Judgment in which not only the living but the dead would find their proper assignment for all eternity.

This quick survey of fact suggests two points: (1) the notion of divine judgment and a Day of Judgment is an essential part of the Hebrew antecedents of Christianity; (2) the Christian conceptions of divine judgment fall into similar categories: a fact encountered in daily life or a great day at the end of history when all will be brought before the throne of God. And we do find both emphases in the New Testament as well as throughout the early church.

III

However strange the notion of a Day of Judgment may seem to us today, it was a familiar center of thought and expectation to our spiritual ancestors, Hebrew and Christian alike.

If Luke deserves to be called "the Gospel of Prayer" because of its emphasis on the prayer life of our Lord, then Matthew deserves to be called "the Gospel of Judgment" because it, even more than the rest, deals with the notion of divine judgment in history and a Day of Judgment at the end of history. This concern of Matthew is not to be wondered at since it is the most Jewish of the Gospels, meaning by that, that it is the most carefully and profoundly related to the Jewish history and phophecy. Touch these anywhere and you touch the live wire of divine judgment. And Matthew devotes two full chapters (24, 25) to our Lord's utterances of divine judgment on the Temple and the world, coupled with stern warnings to the disciples to be ready for the Last Day.

Jesus begins by foretelling the destruction of the Temple because of the disobedience of Israel. Then he gives them a vivid picture of the days ʼimmediately before the Day of Judgment: The faithful will be persecuted; there will be wars and rumors of war; false prophets will be among them; the Temple will be destroyed; the sun will be darkened, the moon will not give her light, the stars will fall. Then—the Son of Man will come with his angels to judge the world.

His disciples are warned to be ready for this day at all times. My old neighbor was true to Matthew: Any day could be Judgment Day. In the parables of the talents, Jesus urges them to invest all they have in time and money for his sake—against his sudden appearing. He tells of the wise and foolish virgins, some of whom were ready for their Lord's coming, some of whom were not—and would be rejected utterly because of it.

Then comes the most famous parable of Judgment ever uttered—known almost lovingly as the "Inasmuch" parable. It may be, as one commentator suggests, a rephrasing of an older Jewish parable—if so, we have no trace of its ancestor. But we do have it—and we need to look at it squarely. What a Day of Judgment it is! The Son of man surrounded by his angels sits on his glorious throne and nations and peoples pass in review. He separates them into two groups: one to be rewarded and one to be punished. It is the "why" of both reward and punishment that brings us up short. "No other piece of Jesus' recorded teachings expresses so eloquently and beautifully the ethical spirit of the Old Testament and Judaism."[3]

The details of this parable are too clearly stated and too well known to require even a simple review. But the underlying ethical convictions need to be faced.

God is good and demands of men a life of righteousness. He is not neutral. He takes sin seriously. He expects obedience in the ordinary, day-to-day relationships of life. He expects His servants to go beyond self and self-service, and to meet the needs of others.

God is no absentee deity—or one given to moral lapses like some Greek god. He is Creator and Judge of the world. No action is too small for Him to miss, nor any too large to deceive Him. He had made known His will to men; He expects them to obey; and He will judge whether they have kept faith with Him or not.

The principle of judgment in the parable is the relationship of people to the law of love and mutual helpfulness. Have people helped those in need? If so, good. If not, too bad.

Two strange and, in a sense, troubling insights are to be found in this parable: (1) some men discover that, although they have not known it, they have been on God's side doing His work, keeping faith with His will all the time; (2) others discover that in waiting around for some striking moment, some great way in which to demonstrate their loyalty to Christ, they have missed the only chance they would ever have to serve Him.

IV

I do not suppose that any parable of our Lord is more deeply disturbing to professedly religious people than this one is—or should be— nor do I know of any that reveals the meaning of Palm Sunday any more completely.

To begin with, the parable puts religious rites and practices in their proper place. They are means, not ends. The true end of obedience is love among men—mutual love and helpfulness among men at the point of need. Church membership, churchgoing, public worship and prayer, mystical experiences—these are good so long as they serve to open our eyes to, deepen our awareness of the reality and meaning of need in human life.

In an old novel, *Miriam's Schooling*, we meet a person called Mrs. Joll who is unpleasant, unkempt, quarrelsome—but whose redeeming quality is this: She comes instantly to the help of anyone—stranger or neighbor—in his illness or need. The novelist says of her, she has done "the one thing which, if ever there is to be a Judgment Day, will put her on the right hand; when all sorts of scientific people, religious people, students of poetry, people with exquisite emotions, will go to the left and be damned everlastingly."[4]

This parable makes it clear that to be good means to be good to someone, to be good for something. Our eloquent prayers, our firm beliefs, our lovely music, our fine sense of fellowship—these are means to the end of an ever deepening outpouring of works of love in life. They must be good for someone, good for something.

V

In a sense the first Palm Sunday was a Day of Judgment—a time which brought the question of loyal love to the foreground and measured people by their obedience to it. Actually it began a week of judgment on the crowds, the critics, and the disciples of our Lord.

It is one thing—and good—to help someone at the point of acute need —but it is quite another to cater to the whims of the crowd. Palm Sunday was a Day of Judgment on crowds and anyone who strives simply to please the crowd. No doubt it was an exhilarating experience to run with the crowd and cry "Hosanna." And, if Jesus had played it smart, as some people think, he would have found out what the crowd wanted and given it to them. But he did not. He learned what we are tempted to forget: You must obey God not man. The crowd may not be right; the crowd may be superficial; the crowd may be hopelessly selfish in what it wants. In which case, the crowd must be ignored or opposed by an invitation to measure itself against the standard of God's will.

Today, occasionally, we hear voices lifted urging the church to find out what the crowd wants and give it to them—or they will cry "Hosanna" around someone else! Those who think this way undoubtedly want the church to fulfill Grover Cleveland's description of a great politician: One who is able to keep both ears to the ground. When I hear the recommendation that we bend and twist the program of the church until it fits this group or that—lest we lose them, fearful thought!—I am surprised that we have not also been urged to join the parade and give S & H Green Stamps to all who come to church or church school! We would surely get a lot of free publicity that way—and might pick up a few lusty-lunged supporters to swell the crowd.

But a crowd—any crowd—never survives a Day of Judgment. Such a day dissolves the crowd because it makes them stand up as persons and answer as individuals regarding their own loyalty, faith, and life. That is what happened to the ones who were shouting their heads off along the road to Jerusalem. When they had to stand up personally and say what they meant, they went off in search of the anonymity of another crowd.

This is not to say we must not be aware of crowds, but it is to say that we should beware of letting the appeal to, or the acclaim of, crowds determine either the policy or program of the church. We are a service organization, true enough, but we exist to serve God and His will for men. He is the center of what we do.

Palm Sunday was a judgment on the critics of our Lord. Finally they had him in their hands. After fretting for months over his teachings and hearing from their spies of his influence, but being unable to get hold of him, they had him in their power. They could either hear him out or silence him. They chose the latter—and thought to do an unusually good job of it by making so vivid a spectacle of his death that other critics would be silenced in advance.

It is a fearful thing to have the freedom, yes, the character, the life of another in our hands—as the critics of our Lord discovered. They were blinded to their holy duty to hear him out. He sealed his fate when he upset the tables of the moneychangers. The authorities moved in and silenced him as best they could.

The Day of Judgment for power is when it is free to exercise its will. The ones who were powerful enough to kill Jesus stand before history as weak, cowardly men, not as men of real power. They were betrayed by such power as they had into thinking they were right. Now we know how wrong they were—even though we continue to seek power, little realizing that the day of power is always a day of judgment.

Palm Sunday was a Day of Judgment for the disciples, too—and continues to be one. They wanted to be optimistic, to be on the winning side. They must have been lifted to seventh heaven when they heard the crowds echo their shouts of acclaim. Soon they were to discover that the triumph that he was seeking was not to come by way of popular acclaim but by way of the agony, the suffering, and the fulfillment of the cross. It is only as we study the cross that we truly see the meaning of the Day of Judgment in Christian thought and life. In its presence, we not only feel the fact of God's judgment but we acknowledge in all humility the justice of it. Thank God, His is a judgment that is rooted and grounded in His heart of love. That is our only hope here and hereafter!

7. Citizens of the Kingdom

MATTHEW 13:44-52, NEW ENGLISH BIBLE

I

The listeners to our Lord's teachings had heard of the kingdom of God all their lives. For generations their fathers had believed in it, prayed for it, and confidently taught their children to anticipate its coming. The kingdom of God had become a commonplace item of their religion—and that was precisely the problem with which Jesus wrestled in many of his parables. He was not trying to get his hearers to believe in the kingdom of God—they did already. He was trying to awaken them to the glorious meaning and worth of that kingdom, and he was trying to tell them that what they had so long expected was actually happening before their very eyes. Of course they did not believe him—not because they doubted the kingdom of God, but because they had become so familiar with it that they no longer thrilled to its glory, or awaited its coming with eager anticipation.

Familiarity does not necessarily breed contempt, but it can and will breed something just as evil unless we are alert to it: casualness, complacency. Sometimes I wonder which is the worse form of blasphemy: to openly doubt and deny that there is a God or to take Him for granted with an air of familiarity. The writer of the book of Job was sure that Job's probing, doubting search for God was much more acceptable to God than was the smug assurance of his friends who not only never doubted God, but professed to have God's thoughts neatly catalogued in their own minds.

We do well to be on our guard lest, through blindness born of familiarity, we lose something of the glory of the Christian faith in the kingdom of God.

Jesus tackled the problem squarely—give him credit for that—but, as every teacher knows, few things are harder than to breathe new life into an ancient or hallowed idea. Both his aim and the method he used can help us to a new awareness of the meaning of the divine event called Easter.

What he did was quite simple: so simple that once it was done, there was no argument about it. The matter was settled.

II

It was an axiom of Jewish thought in Jesus' day that God would create the kingdom, locate it on earth, in Palestine to be exact, with Jerusalem as the capital. The Jews as the Chosen People would be the citizens of it. The bonds of oppression would be thrown off—finally they would be free from Greek, Roman, and Egyptian threats. All nations would look to this kingdom, this city, and this people for guidance.

Like the prophets before him, Jesus saw what was wrong with this present dream. The ones who believed it never once asked whether they were fit for citizenship in the kingdom—they simply assumed they were! "Not so," said Jesus.

The kingdom of heaven is like treasure lying buried in a field. The man who found it, buried it again; and for sheer joy went and sold everything he had, and bought that field.

Here is another picture of the kingdom of Heaven. A merchant looking out for fine pearls found one of very special value; so he went and sold everything he had, and bought it.

Again the kingdom of Heaven is like a net let down into the sea, where fish of every kind were caught in it. When it was full, it was dragged ashore. Then the men sat down and collected the good fish into pails and threw the worthless away. That is how it will be at the end of time. The angels will go forth, and they will separate the wicked from the good, and throw them into the blazing furnace, the place of wailing and grinding of teeth.

Have you understood all this? he asked; and they answered, Yes. He said to them, When, therefore, a teacher of the law has become a learner in the kingdom of Heaven, he is like a householder who can produce from his store both the new and the old (Matt. 13:44-52, NEB).

I am sure his listeners got the point that men must not merely discover the kingdom, but in order to own it, or possess it, or be citizens in it, they must accept it as the only really important thing in their lives and be willing to give everything else for the infinite privilege of living in it.

It is as though we were on a journey, he said, and chanced to discover a great treasure hidden and forgotten in some field. We would buy that field even if we had to sell all else that we possessed in order to get it. Or it is as though we were a lover of pearls and chanced one day to see the perfect pearl. We would gladly sell all else that we had in order to possess it.

Finding and possessing the kingdom of God is something like this, Jesus warned his hearers. We may stumble on to it by accident or chance, but we cannot own or possess it except we lay all else on the line as its purchase price. And it is worth all that we have—and more too, more than we can ever get or hope to get.

This emphasis of our Lord upon the need for complete commitment to the will of God if we are to be fit citizens of the kingdom of God amounts to a refrain in all his teachings. It sounds through the Sermon on the Mount as he outlines the duties of discipleship.

If you would live in the kingdom of God, he told his disciples, you must live in perfect obedience to God's will. You must conquer hate, lust, anger, and greed. You must subordinate property to service and need. You must trust God so completely that there will be no room for either fear or anxiety in your life. You must meet curses with prayers and vengeance with forgiveness. Then, and only then, he said, will you be ready to enter into and possess the kingdom of God.

Upon another occasion, Jesus was stopped by one whom we have come to know as "the rich young ruler." This man wanted the most important thing open to a human being—the gift of eternal life. "What must I do to inherit eternal life?" was the way he put the question to our Lord. Jesus studied him for a moment, then said, "You know the law and the commandments, don't you?" "Yes," was the reply, "I have kept them all my life." Something in his manner conveyed his great spiritual need to Jesus who "looked on him and loved him" as he threw open the door of the kingdom to him. "One thing more you must do," Jesus said. "You must get rid of all that separates you from God. Go, sell all that you have and give it to the poor." Stop getting; start giving. Only those who have mastered the art of giving can receive the precious gifts of God. You must learn how to give lovingly to those in need and give as long as you have anything to give. Then and only then will you be so empty of pride, greed, desire, and anxiety about the future that the love of God can truly enter in and take full possession of you, bringing with it the gift of eternal life.

It was a hard choice—far harder than any we consciously meet—and the young man just could not carry through on his high dream: "He went away sorrowing, because he had great possessions." His involvement in the world was so deep that he simply could not sell all that he had in order to possess the pearl of great price—even eternal life in the kingdom of God.

I might as well confess that I have always been puzzled by that word in the New Testament which tells us that "the common people heard him gladly." I am convinced that that claim needs to be revised in the light of the Gospel records themselves. It would be far truer to fact if it could be enlarged to read: "The common people heard him gladly until they understood what he meant; then, like the rich young ruler, they went away sorrowing, for all of them were involved in many things they did not want to give up in order to follow him, or to enter the kingdom, or to possess eternal life." Jesus was met by a mounting wall of incredulity and unbelief throughout his public ministry—that is a fact beyond dispute. Yet he talked to his own people about ideas, hopes, and dreams they had embraced for generations. With this difference: He blinded them by a vision of their glory and frightened them by a frank statement of what must be done by any who would claim them.

III

I get the distinct impression that we handle Christmas, Good Friday, and Easter much as the contemporaries of our Lord did the idea of the kingdom of God—with a familiarity that borders on casualness and complacency. We take them so for granted that the brightness of their glory is all but lost. This fact reminds me of something that happened during the General Conference of the Methodist Church held in Minneapolis, Minnesota, in April, 1956.

We were meeting in the auditorium and the delegates were assigned seats facing a huge platform. On that platform was a big cross flanked by two equally large candelabra. The cross was composed of opaque glass which covered fluorescent tubes that lighted the entire cross. Soon after the conference opened, a delegate sent up this request to the presiding officer: "Dim the cross; it hurts our eyes."

Some of us found ourselves hoping and praying that that would not prove to be prophetic of the spirit of the conference itself.

When the glory of something like Easter dazzles us, bewilders us, even frightens us, we either turn away from it or seek to dim it until it is more easily bearable. But before we do this, let us take a good look at Easter even if it dazzles and hurts us. What is Easter and what does it mean?

Several answers suggest themselves to the question, "What is Easter?"

The most obvious one is also the truest one: Easter is the historic celebration of the resurrection of Jesus Christ. The New Testament admits of no doubt on this point. We have snatches and fragments of the first sermons of the first preachers of the Christian Church in our book of Acts and in Paul's letters. Hear what they say about it: "But God raised him up" (Acts 2:24). "This Jesus God raised up, and of that we all are witnesses" (Acts 2:32). ". . . whom God raised from the dead. To this we are witnesses" (Acts 3:15).

Paul wrote the letters to the Corinthians scarcely twenty-five years after the resurrection, and said,

For I delivered to you as of first importance what I also received, that Christ died for our sins in accordance with the scriptures, that he was buried, that he was raised on the third day in accordance with the scriptures, and that he appeared to Cephas, then to the twelve. Then he appeared to more than five hundred brethren at one time. . . . Then he appeared to James, then to all the apostles. Last of all, as to one untimely born, he appeared also to me (I Cor. 15:3-8).

People who like a tidy story which contains no problems or ambiguities will turn away from a casual reading of the Gospel narratives about the resurrection because they do not give us a coherent, convincing, step-by-step account of what happened. But it would be unforgivably superficial to let this fact of disunity in the reports blind us to the unquestioned unity among them on the fact that they were trying to describe: namely, their experience of the risen Lord.

These preachers of the early church used this experienced fact of the risen Lord as proof of three tremendous claims: (1) that he was the Messiah; (2) that God through him had overcome sin and death; (3) that whoever would rise with him must first die with him.

IV

It is not too much to say that the early church is a reaction to this fact of the risen Lord. Not that the early Christians understood all that it meant, much less agreed among themselves on some pat interpretations of it. But they stood firmly on the fact that even as others had experienced the risen Lord, so had they. Of this they were called to be witnesses. That is why the church has always thought of itself as a witnessing fellowship.

There are many ways of describing what the resurrection of Christ, this experience of the risen Lord which shines with dazzling brightness through the New Testament, came to mean to the early Christians as well as to subsequent generations. It clinched the Christian case which sought to present the life and teachings of our Lord as a full revelation of God's will for man. It was God's stamp of approval on all that Jesus had said and done. Without it, death had the final word on life. With it, life—the life of God—had the final word on death.

The experience of the risen Lord opened the door to a new life for man in God. Sin could be overcome. Death could be conquered. Man could become a new creature in Christ—for the power of God had proved it to be so!

This experience of the risen Lord pointed the way to the abundant life here and the eternal life which stretched beyond the experience of death. Death was no longer an end; it was the beginning of a spiritual journey to the very heart of the love of God.

Some may want to make more specific claims than others feel they can about the resurrection, but let us beware of dimming the glory of it. Let us beware of treating it so familiarly that we turn away from the hidden treasure in it, from the pearl of great price it is. Rather let us with joy in our hearts be ready to sell all else that we have in order to possess it. But we must be ready to sell all else and hold back nothing.

V

In 1938 the missionary forces of the Christian churches of the world met in Jerusalem to discuss the role of missions in the modern world. Among the many things said upon that occasion one stands out. "A profound change has come over the motivation of missions in our times," the delegates said. "Formerly we were stirred by the thought that people were dying without Christ; now we are moved by the thought that people are living without him."

Does anyone doubt that many live and die as though Jesus Christ had never lived, died, and risen again? We shrink from the hard discovery that we must be willing to leave all and follow him if we are to know him at all. Yet this is a discovery which we need to make today because we live in a time when cheap substitutes for vital faith may be bought at any price on any bargain counter. This discovery of the all-or-none character of the Christian commitment is so significant that it ought to be stated in a number of ways lest we miss its supreme importance for our life:

1. If our religious faith is going to mean anything to us, it must mean everything to us.

2. If we try to limit religion to a part of our life, we will lose it throughout the whole of our life.

3. We do not get, we cannot get a vital Christian faith as we might collect a roomful of antiques—piece by piece; a vital faith is a living unit that we either get all at once or we never get at all. To be sure, it may be as immature as an embryo when we get it and be in need of careful nurture before it achieves full powers, but even an embryo is a living unit or it has no future as a part of life.

4. We cannot buy a vital Christian faith on margin—on margin of our time or possession or life; we either lay everything we have on the line, or we waste what we do put there.

5. We cannot win a vital Christian experience by means of a calculating and cautious and prudential approach; we fall in love without reservation—or we miss it altogether.

6. In only a very limited sense is it true that in religion we get out of it what we put into it. In simple fact, we must put everything into it in order to get anything out of it; if we put anything less than everything into it, we get nothing out of it but the shame of hypocrisy, a sense of frustration, and an experience of profound disillusionment.

I am not telling you anything new when I say that this sort of presentation of the claim of great faith has had a rough time of it in the modern world—until almost yesterday. Most of us simply do not want to pay that kind of price for religious faith—or for anything else. By and large, we hope to pick it up at a cut-rate price at some pious bargain counter. For until almost yesterday, we were sure we could work out our own salvation without fear and without too much trembling. But as a result of a terrible hammering of the last thirty years, we are so afflicted by fear and trembling that we have almost lost faith in our ability to do anything about our own salvation.

We can, if we desire, put our spiritual plight in terms of a single cutting sentence: We are citizens of an age that seems determined to write its obituary in terms of evasions rather than affirmations, of compromises rather than convictions. It is to us, therefore, that the historic Christian faith turns with its word of sharp warning, yet of strong hope: *You must come to terms with God as we see Him in Christ! It is His way or your way—and between them you must choose.* There is no compromise! It is all or none. It is all His way or none His way. We choose to travel the whole of His way—or we do not even make a beginning.

I am well aware of the fact this all-or-none character of the Christian challenge has awakened criticism and protest in many quarters. I have heard it called many things, the milder epithets being "sheer bigotry," "stark prejudice," "blatant dogmatism."

But, as a matter of fact, it is none of these. It is simply the logical conclusion to the teachings of Jesus Christ and to his insight into the nature of the will of God for human life and into the experience of the risen Lord which we commemorate on Easter. The only way to alter that conclusion is to remove Jesus Christ as the historic revelation of the will of God for the life of man. Then and only then can we remove or modify the all-or-none character of the Christian challenge. But keep Jesus Christ—and we keep the challenge. I do not know of anyone who thinks he can remove Jesus Christ from Christianity and keep even the semblance of Christianity in our religious faith.

This severe choice between God's will and our will runs all through the New Testament. And the parable with which we began represents a beautiful statement of it. If we want the hidden treasure in the field, if we want the pearl of great price, we must be willing with joy in our hearts to sell all that we have in order to purchase it. We may discover it by accident, but we can possess it only when we are willing to lay all that we have on the altar of complete devotion to the will of God as we see it in Jesus Christ.

8. Devils Love a Vacuum

MATTHEW 12:38-50

I

The management of evil begins as a deeply personal problem. Everyone must face it and win the victory if his life is to know any sense of abundance and fulfillment.

How clearly Jesus saw this. Few of his parables are more pertinent to our time than the one in which he illustrates the right and the wrong way to conquer the centers of evil in our lives. Cast in the thought-patterns of his time when everyone believed in demons and demon-possession, the parable tells of a man who has successfully ousted a demon from his life. Overjoyed to be free, he sweeps and polishes the house of his life, but leaves it empty. The evicted spirit wanders around for awhile, gets tired of being without a home, and returns. He finds his former home not only unoccupied but even more desirable than it had ever been before—so back he comes—but not alone! He gets seven other devils even worse than he to move in with him. And, as Jesus says, "The last state of that man becomes worse than the first."

Study this parable for a moment and we come up with four affirmations that suggest a way of dealing with some of the major difficulties that are besetting us today—providing we have the courage, hope, faith, and strength to take it. In effect, these affirmations constitute the Christian alternative to chaos.

The first affirmation can be phrased this way: *Life abhors a vacuum.* We know this to be true of the physical world. We can create vacuums, to be sure, and have done so repeatedly, but they must be small and carefully handled. All the power and weight of the universe is pushing in on them, seeking to destroy them.

Furthermore, it is common knowledge that life abhors a social vacuum. Put a group of children who are strangers to each other together and watch them for awhile. If you do not give them a game to play, they will soon invent or agree upon one and play it with heart and soul. That is the nature of children; they must play, and play they will somewhere, somehow, with someone. Just so it is in the nature of a group of people like ourselves that we shall have a government of some kind or other. And there are different kinds of governments, ranging from tyranny to democracy. Put a group of us in proximity with one another for a period of time and some sort of community organization will evolve. Life simply fills up a social vacuum.

Life has just as little patience with a spiritual vacuum. It is idle talk to say as some parents do say, "We are not going to try to indoctrinate our children. We are going to let them decide for themselves what they want to believe in religion." If this should mean that we are not going to make them intolerant and dogmatic about religious beliefs, well and good. But it seldom means that. What is really meant is the utterly dangerous notion that we are not going to teach them anything at all. Try that, and we will find them getting their instructions from someone else. Children will think about religion, they will ask questions about it, and they will seek instruction regarding it. This teaching will come either from parents who care and understand or from others who may not care and may not understand. To live is to believe in something! And life fills in with a vengeance every attempt to create a spiritual vacuum, even though we bless it by the title of "broad-mindedness."

William Butler Yeats has given this eloquent and penetrating description of what has happened to the recent attempt to create a spiritual vacuum in our civilization:

> Things fall apart; the center cannot hold;
> Mere anarchy is loosed upon the world;
> The best lack all conviction, while the worst
> Are full of passionate intensity.[1]

Something like that invariably happens when we try to live in a spiritual vacuum. Life demands and will have something at its center— some ideal to which it can give itself with "passionate intensity." It may be a low ideal of country, race, or class, or a high ideal of a com-

munity of nations and the brotherhood of man. It can be a cheap ideal
in which we profit at the expense of others, or it may be a high and
costly ideal in which the necessities of life are shared with the people
who need them.

I am sure I will not need to point up to this generation the moral of
this parable as it applies to the life of the totalitarian regimes of the
modern world. They emerged in a chaos of conflicting purposes that
surrounded the life of the people who embraced them. The
countries that embraced these regimes first fought them off, but, being
unable to find any other answer to the chaos that threatened, accepted
them. It really does not matter whether we make the case study in
Fascist countries of the recent past or in present Communism regimes.
The tale is the same: Nature abhors a vacuum, a lack of purpose, a
lack of loyalty to some great cause in the life of any people.

There is a measure of truth in the statement that the rise of Communism has been in exact proportion to man's loss of faith in himself
and God. And there is at least as much truth in the suspicion that our
faith in atomic weapons is in direct proportion to our loss of faith in
ourselves and in God.

So each in his own way can join his testimony with that of the man
in the parable that, in its broad ranges, life abhors a vacuum and sets
about filling it at once and with the materials at hand.

II

The second affirmation of the parable grows out of the fact that the
man was content when he had evicted the Devil; he put nothing else
in his place. He was not only free, he was empty. *He soon learned
that negations are not enough.* This cuts to the heart of the religious
problem of many of us today. We are nihilists. We see "No Exit." We
feel no importance in meanings and purposes. I am not half as concerned about what men do not believe as about what they do believe
and why they believe it. We are not going to find our way out of the
dangerous period in which we live by believing in nothing. Our survival
and salvation depend upon our believing the right thing and believing
it with every fiber of our being. Too many of us are adept at reciting
what we do not believe, but what is it that we do believe? It is not
especially difficult to take apart an inherited creed, any creed. Most
of us can do that—have done it, in fact.

Professor Walter Kaufmann of Princeton University did this in a brilliant way in an article in *Harper's Magazine* some years ago. He called it, "The Faith of a Heretic." (A more accurate title would have been "The Faithlessness of a Heretic.") Professor Kaufmann tells in a fascinating way what he does not believe, why he does not believe it, but when he gets around to saying what he does believe in, why he believes in it, and what he proposes to do about it, he has little to say. This is no personal criticism of Professor Kaufmann; he but exemplifies in a brilliant way the situation that all too many of us are content with: We like to take things apart; we are reluctant to try to put them together.

Take the great creeds of Christendom: Anyone who is acquainted with their genealogy knows that they are human and earthy in origin and development. They come to us bearing the marks not alone of the ages in which they were born, but also of the ages that have cherished them before they have been given to us. It is easy to point out inconsistency, incredulity, and sometimes simple superstitions, either explicitly or implicitly stated in these creeds. But the real test of our spiritual capacity is not the ability to take a creed apart; it is the ability to put one together.

We learned in our infancy a lesson which we should not have forgotten in our maturity: It is far, far easier to knock something down that to build it up. As infants, we came equipped with the convulsive movement of hand and foot which easily topples a pile of blocks. But we early found it a quite different matter to take one block after another and build a pyramid. We had to learn how to do that! In similar fashion, we are good at saying what we do not believe, but we stumble and stutter over what we do believe. Yet we shall not find our way out of the confusion in which we live until we are able to do just that.

There must be something at the center of our mind that persuades our reason and understanding—something to which we can give the full consent of our intelligence if religion is to be a power for good in our lives. We must be prepared to state our faith as confidently as ever our fathers said, "I believe in God the Father Almighty. . . ." We must be able to say what it is we believe.

Let us always hope that we learn from the errors of dogmatism and never try to freeze our beliefs at any given point and say, in effect, "This is all I am ever going to believe." That would be disastrous, too.

But let us remember that there must be a solid nucleus of rational conviction at the center of our religion if it is to persuade our mind, if we are to be able to live by it and to share it with others. Negations, of themselves, are chaos, not an alternative to chaos. Alternatives will be built, if they are built, out of affirmations, and they must command the full consent of our mind and spirit.

We are beginning to recognize that negations are not enough. Some years ago, Van Wyck Brooks saw this as he sought to understand what was going on in the spiritual life of our times. He revealed the deep hopes of mankind when he wrote, "I see on all sides a hunger for affirmations, for a world without confusion, waste or gropings, a world that is full of order and purpose."[2] When we think about the hazardous future we face, we keep up our courage by saying, "There must be some way out." Time and again I have heard the young people who will bear responsibilities in this and the next generation ask, "Isn't there some way out, even if it is a new way?"

It is at this point that the Christian alternative to chaos comes into sharp focus. It is far from negative. It bears the names: "the kingdom of God," "the human family," or any one of a half dozen other designations which indicate our belief in and loyalty to a purpose not our own, which threads life and history. For the Christian, this is the light by which he sees, the path on which he walks, the goal he seeks to serve.

III

The third insight of this parable calls attention to the fact that the evicted devil took full advantage of the unoccupied and refurbished life and moved back in, not alone this time but with the terrifying support of seven other devils all worse than he. This, in translation, suggests that evil always replaces itself with evil. Fear never replaces itself with trust. Hatred never replaces itself with love. Such qualities replace themselves with their own kind, only worse, when left to themselves. We cannot drive fear out of the world by depending on instruments which engender fear in everyone else. The more we try to terrorize others, the more fearful we become. We live and breathe in an atmosphere of fear these days because we are trying to become so strong that other people will be afraid of what we might do in case we are displeased with what they do. So we talk about the necessity of having in being so vast and so far flung a web of massive retaliation that we will be able to destroy anyone who threatens our existence.

At the World Order Study Conference in Cleveland, Ohio, in November 1958 a cold-blooded physicist, well acquainted with nuclear weapons, told the assembled churchmen that new weapons have reached a state of effectiveness where one might safely say that there is no longer any real advantage in a surprise attack. No surprise attack could be so thorough as to rule out the possibility of at least partial retaliation, which with these weapons would be equivalent to annihilation. Were you startled, as I was, when Dr. Gordon Lapp, formerly with the Atomic Energy Commission, said that we ought to suspend the manufacture of A-bombs at Oak Ridge because we now have a large enough stockpile to kill every Russian twenty-five times over?

It is hard to believe that such dreadful instruments of destruction not only are in existence but are being stock-piled at various places on this earth's surface for the purpose of exterminating people like ourselves.

All of which amounts to a plain admission that fear is on the march and is breeding true to itself not only in our own life but in the lives of other people. Time and again we have seen the United States Congress hurry through a bill which appropriates billions upon billions for military defense and then haggle endlessly over the millions that are going to be spent in foreign aid of nonmilitary character.

How long will it be before we accept the simple fact that we are trying to live in a world that is dead? An age that is gone beyond recall, that has written its concluding words in terms of the threat of annihilating mankind? We cannot resurrect that world, but we can die with it. Thank God, an increasing number of men do not want to bring back the old world, nor do we want to retain any of the remnants of it, nor do we see the necessity of dying with it. Convinced that evil always replaces itself with evil, we are midwifing a new world into existence.

IV

Clearly, there must be a new strategy if we are going to avoid the fate of the man in the Master's parable. And that new strategy is suggested by the fourth conclusion of the parable, namely, the man should have placed something good, creative, positive in his life to take the place of the ousted demon. In no other way could he have hoped to keep free from its clutches. In other words, overcome evil with good. That is the only way we can overcome evil; every other known way merely multiplies it. It is the standing obligation of the Christian faith to overcome evil and by the only known way: the doing of good, not in abstract terms, not even in good intentions alone, though these are essential, but more concretely in terms of the support of the United Nations, the program of UNESCO, the encouragement of groups like the National and World Councils of Churches to address themselves with vigor and realism to problems we face today. It is at this point that many of us lose heart. Forgetting that the road to hell is paved with good intentions, that a little learning is a dangerous thing, we seek for halfway houses along the route. In fact, our generation is looking for a kind of halfway-house Christianity, a version of the Christian faith that will enable us to do as little as necessary in order to be saved, but stops far short of full commitment and full consecration.

We find this to be true in the life and work of the local church. This may sound like a paradox, but the ones who weaken the church the most are not those who openly oppose it, but those who support it in a half-hearted way.

This sort of loyalty is not enough. Unless there is an affirmative, aggressive loyalty to the church in the life of an individual, unless he does something to nurture and bear witness to this loyalty, it will wither and die. We ought to probe deeply into the question of our steward-ship in the church. How hard have we worked at being a faithful member? Have we been content to give the church as little as possible rather than eager to give her as much as we can? If we have given little, we have not only weakened the church, we have robbed ourselves of whatever strength the church might give us.

The answer to little faith is greater faith; the answer to a feeling of separation from the church is to become ever more deeply involved in the life of the church. The church needs us—but no worse than we need the church.

In similar fashion on a world scale it is not enough simply to be afraid of the future; we must address ourselves to the task of building the kind of a future in which there is no need for fear. This is a matter in which every man can participate. There is room and need for the housewife, the professional man, and the international diplomat. The only way to avoid being overwhelmed by a sevenfold invasion of devils is to address ourselves to those things which bring courage, hope, and confidence in ourselves and in the future. The faint-hearted, the quitters, and the cry-babies will shrink from this sort of prospect; the church that would serve our Lord in days like these must "come to him prepared for a hard campaign."

Evil can be overcome—evil, in the concrete forms of hunger, suspicion, hatred, and strife. But it can be overcome only by good—good, in the concrete forms of food, trust, justice, love, and security. The only way to overcome evil is with good. Every other way will multiply in number and increase in viciousness the evils which now inhabit the life of mankind.

V

Thomas Chalmers, the great Scottish Divine, was making the same general point in his greatest sermon, entitled, "The Expulsive Power of a New Affection." He says that we can overcome evil with good. Once we learn to love God with all of our heart, soul, mind, and strength and let this become the organizing center of our attitude toward other people and toward our own life, we have installed good rather than evil at the center of our being. To put it humbly, we have opened the door of our life and have let God move in as a saving fact, one upon whom we can rely in even the most desperate situation, whom we can love no matter what happens. As this love for God broadens and deepens, it literally becomes a dominate factor in life, expelling the demons of doubt, fear, and guilt. There is nothing automatic about this process; it requires constant attention of one who is seeking to love God and to serve Him. It requires the courage to start over again after we have failed in our determination to be faithful. But as we persist, we shall find that our latter state is much better than the former one.

Jesus saw that every man will serve some master whether it be God or Mammon. He confronted his hearers with the requirement to choose the one they would serve. This choice is still before every human being. Who is the Lord of our life? What is it we love with all our heart, soul, mind, and strength: God or something other than God?

Samuel Longfellow learned and put in verse a lesson we can all afford to study, namely, freedom, joy, and love come through perfect obedience, perfect loyalty to God.

> Holy spirit, right divine,
> King within my conscience Reign;
> Be my Lord, and I shall be
> Firmly bound, forever free.

9. Wanted: Special Messengers!

LUKE 16:19-31

I

God expects us to be immediately and completely compassionate in the presence of human need. This ancient truth of religious faith never grows old in the telling. And it surprises all of us in the arms of a complacent attitude toward human need. This is the point of our Lord's parable of the rich man and the beggar. And we find it displayed, as a precious jewel, in a setting that makes its truth live with renewed vigor and brilliance.

It sets forth a theme that is as old and as universal as mankind: the contrast between the rich man and the beggar, and the ultimate reversal of their fortunes. It warns that there will come a time when "the last shall be first, and the first shall be last."

Ordinary people have always longed and loved to see the proud man get his due—as he surely does in this parable. Yet we should be careful not to mistake the intent of the parable at this point. It is neither a blanket condemnation of the rich man nor an exaltation of the beggar. Rather it is a condemnation of the self-centered love, the blindness of the rich man to the realities of God's will in the presence of human need. And that condemnation is etched in every line of the story— and it still stands as a warning to men who live that way.

II

There are two acts in the story: one located on earth and the other in twin scenes of bliss and torment after death.

The earthly scene was familiar to those who heard the parable. Beggars were posted at every vantage point in city and country: the

71

gates of the city, the gates of the Temple, the gates of the royal court, and the gates of the wealthy and powerful. If the beggar could walk, hobble, or crawl, he usually went where he wanted to go under his own power. But if he were completely helpless—as in this case—his friends would carry him to his post, leave him for their work, and return to take him home at the end of the day. As Lazarus lay there, he was the epitome of helpless, hopeless human need—unable to defend himself from sun, beast, or man.

The rich man must have known Lazarus was there. He could not help seeing the beggar each time he went in and out of his house. He knew and respected Lazarus' right to be there—religious law both protected the poor who sought alms and enjoined almsgiving as a duty on the rich and the pious. The rich man may have instructed his servants to feed Lazarus each day with what was left over from his own table— which, we may safely surmise, was more than crumbs. There is no reason to doubt that the rich man gave alms to Lazarus and his friends in full accordance with the requirements of the law.

But—and this is the point of Scene One—the rich man really never *saw* Lazarus as a human being, as a needy person, as a child of God who was in desperate need of help that he alone could give. *He saw Lazarus as a beggar, not as a man, certainly not as a brother.* Whatever he did for him was done out of what was left after he had had all he wanted—food, money, or time. Like the rich men who gave great gifts to the Temple "out of their plenty," what this rich man gave Lazarus did not hurt him a bit. His gifts cost him no food, no pleasure, no time, no comfort. He took care—good care—of himself first; and undoubtedly made excellent provision for similar care of his own family, for he had five brothers living with or near him.

Had someone reproached the rich man for his behavior he would have been astounded and offended. Was he not giving Lazarus food? Was he not fulfilling the law? Was he not doing as much for the beggar at his gate as any others were doing for the beggars at their gates? Had he not made the money he was spending on himself or giving away? Was he not entitled to spend it as he pleased—where it would give him the greatest pleasure and comfort? So long as he fulfilled the letter of the law which ordered him to give alms to the beggar, did he not have the moral and religious right to do as he pleased with the rest?

Now the parable shifts to the second setting—with a staggering reversal in fortunes. Lazarus died and was taken by angels to "the bosom of Abraham"—the symbol of bliss for the Jew. Much as the Negro spirituals and Gospel songs long to be "safe in the arms of Jesus," the faithful Jew looked to life with the great Father of the Hebrews—Abraham. The rich man died and was buried and went to the place of torment called Hades.

In the folklore of Judaism, the places of bliss and torment, while close together, were separated by a gulf no one could cross. Dives, the rich man, sees Abraham caring tenderly for Lazarus. He accepts the justice of it all; at least, he does not cry out to high heaven against it. He asks only that Lazarus be permitted to bring the least amount of comfort conceivable—a drop of water on his finger tips—to cool his raging thirst. Whereas Lazarus in life had begged for crumbs of bread, now Dives in death begs for drops of water—with this difference: Lazarus got the crumbs, but the drops of water were denied. The explanation of this is twofold: Dives had his comfort and Lazarus his anguish in life; now each is experiencing what he missed in life. In addition, the great gulf between them now cannot be crossed. Whereas Dives could have helped Lazarus on earth, now neither Lazarus nor Abraham may help Dives should they desire to do so.

The rich man accepts the justice of this hard explanation without curse or cavil. He then thinks of his brothers and asks that Lazarus be sent to warn them of what lies ahead. "No," says Abraham, "they have Moses and the prophets to warn them; let them hear them!"

But the man in torment had had Moses and the prophets, too, and look where he was! He knew how casually his brothers treated Moses and the prophets. He pleaded that one who came from the dead might shock them into listening. "No," said Abraham. "If they do not hear Moses and the prophets, neither will they be convinced if some one should rise from the dead."

III

It is not hard to see why this parable was treasured by the early church. The church was composed of people—Jew and Gentile alike—who passionately believed in Jesus Christ, in his resurrection and saving power. They could not understand why the ones who had heard Jesus preach, who had actually known him, had not accepted him as the Messiah and Lord. They were convinced that his coming had been anticipated and foretold by Moses and the prophets—yet the ones who knew Moses and the prophets best (the scribes and the Pharisees) were the very ones who not only rejected him but engineered his death. And these same worthies had scoffed at the disciples' witness to his resurrection.

This parable must have explained much to the early church: how the very ones who had Moses and the prophets paid no attention to them—hence the scribes and the Pharisees were not really expecting the Messiah and therefore rejected Jesus; that should one be so blind he will not be guided by Moses and the prophets, he would not listen to One who rose from the dead, as Jesus had done, to no avail so far as the scribes and the Pharisees were concerned.

The parable is based squarely on the world view common to the Jews of Jesus' day. The places of bliss and torment, the evening in the afterlife of unjust fortune in this life, the possibility of seeing and talking across the fixed gulf between bliss and torment, the unalterability of the divine decree as to where a man should go, and the adequacy of Moses and the prophets for life here and hereafter—these emphases were accepted with little question by Jesus and his hearers.

There is no mistaking the realism and the genius with which Jesus weaves these into his story. By the turn of a word, he opens one window after another into the recesses of motive and deed until, as Dr. George A. Buttrick says, "We are left 'unmasked and defenseless.' "

This parable is another document in support of the claim that Jesus "knew what was in man," knew us from the inside out, in motive, desire, and deed.

Here we see our blindness to the divine meanings of ordinary things. We live life as though it were a horizontal, a two-dimensional affair. We move among people and things, people and cars, people and buildings, so continuously, so thoughtlessly that our awareness of people as persons fades out and, except by an act of will, we no longer separate people from things; *in fact, people become things.* It is human, I know —terribly, tragically human—to become so accustomed to the sight of a beggar at our door that the awareness of his need no longer goes through us like a knife. It is not until our eyes are freed from blinders by sufferings of our own that we actually feel the sufferings of others who have been around us all the time, and in need of help that we could give.

To me, the most pathetic scene in *King Lear* finds the old king wandering about the heath seeking shelter from the violent storm that has just burst upon his head. For the first time in his life, he realized what storms like these mean to those wretches who must live on the heath all the time. He cries:

> Poor naked wretches, whereso'er you are,
> That bide the pelting of this pitiless storm,
> How shall your houseless heads and unfed sides,
> Your looped and windowed raggedness, defend you
> From seasons such as these? O! I have ta'en
> Too little care of this.[1]

So it was with the rich man in the parable. Not until pain had purified his vision was he able to see and feel the pain that had lain unseen on his very doorstep day after day all the time. Our inhumanity to each other—born of callousness and insensitivity rather than open malice—has never received a more eloquent statement than in this parable.

Here we see what can only be called the helplessness of God in the presence of choices we may make. Loving Lazarus and Dives equally, God could not bring them into a relationship of loving helpfulness either here or hereafter. He could not open the eyes of Dives to the needs of Lazarus in time to allay the sufferings of the beggar. Nor could He permit Lazarus to ease the sufferings of Dives later on. Which, as I understand it, is a way of saying that we are dealing with God and He is trying to break through to us in all our dealings with each other. What to the casual eye seemed a daily affair in which a rich man passed unfeelingly by a suffering beggar was occurring, in reality, against a backdrop of the compassionate love and judgment of Almighty God. Both the rich man and Lazarus later could have cried with Jacob of old, "Surely the Lord was here and I knew it not!"

It is risky business to say or think that God can be blocked out of any phase of life. The only safe thing to do is to be guided by the hard-won wisdom of others that he is everywhere as Judge and Father. But to say this is not to compromise our freedom and responsibility. We can continue to walk by the sufferings of others with averted or veiled eyes and insulated spirits. But if we choose to live that way, God cannot force us to change—until it is too late to change.

Not even a special messenger will turn the trick—though the rich man thought it might! He pleaded that his brethren would not pay any more attention to Moses and the prophets than he had done, and therefore begged that Lazarus be sent to warn them.

It is in answer to this request that we all but stumble over one of the most critical if not downright skeptical valuations of man found in the New Testament. Abraham says it would do no good to send Lazarus back, for "if they do not hear Moses and the prophets, neither will they be convinced if some one would rise from the dead."

IV

The parable takes a dim view of the value of special messengers. Yet the request for such is a continuing staple in religion—even in our own time. The Pharisees listened to Jesus' teachings and said, "Show us a sign. Do something special and spectacular. Don't just talk about brotherhood and love—we've heard all that before. Perform some great miracle; then we will believe that you are the Messiah!" The New Testament records the simple fact that even when they saw the miracle, they continued to disbelieve. *It takes more than a miracle to cure insensitivity and to nurture faith.*

Nor were the Pharisees alone in this desire for special proof. The disciples felt the need of it too. According to John, near the end of Jesus' ministry Thomas and Philip were seeking additional reassurances to bolster their sagging faith: Was he really the Son of God? Was he God's word for man? So Philip said, "Lord show us the Father, and we will be satisfied." Jesus answered, "Have I been with you so long, and yet you do not know me, Philip? He who has seen me has seen the Father; how can you say, 'Show us the Father'? Do you not believe that I am in the Father and the Father in me?"

The relationship between special events, miracles, special messengers and increase in faith is not reassuring. Though the disciples preached the resurrection, said they had seen Jesus alive after death, Jew and Greek alike scoffed at them. The Pharisees were content to spread the rumor that the disciples had stolen his body from the grave. It comes down to something quite simple and very ordinary, doesn't it? The materials necessary to an awareness of ultimate truths lie all around us all the time. We need "no opening skies, no angel visitant," no special messenger. And if we cannot see these truths in ordinary events, there is a good chance we will not see them in other events, no matter how extraordinary they are.

As a matter of hard fact, this parable may be taken as a firm warning to Christians not to rely on miracles and special messengers in the preaching of the gospel. This warning needs to be raised with regularity, for there is something pathetic about the way religious people look to such spectacular hopes. During the last century members of a religious cult called the Millerites used to gather with regularity on some appointed hill or other to be on hand when Christ returned. As the set time came and went, without any such occurrence, the fanatical leaders would scan their biblical charts again and come up with the belated but obvious revelation that they had miscalculated by a few years—and the weary, disillusioned people would scatter to their homes until told when and where to assemble again.

Surely there is a moral in all this for the church today when we are invited to rally around one great evangelist after another: Moody, Sunday, Graham. Without depreciating in the least the value of the efforts of these men, it is imperative to keep in mind that the enduring worth of their efforts is measured by the degree to which they result in or gear in with stable social institutions. Moody's great efforts spurred the spread of the Sunday schools and to some extent the Y.M.C.A. and thus contributed to the rapidly expanding emphasis on religious education on all levels. Billy Sunday's efforts tied in with very little and are now mostly forgotten. Certainly their contribution to the Christian Church is negligible. It is too early—and I have no desire to attempt—to pass judgment on the long-range effects of the efforts of Billy Graham.

As of now, the Graham crusades have meant little to the churches and nothing at all to the spread of an intelligent approach to and understanding of the Bible. Ruling out of consideration for the moment the high moral character and intense religious zeal of Billy Graham—for whom I have the highest personal regard—the most obvious tangible result of his campaigns to date has been an encouragement of an indefensible biblical literalism and theological fundamentalism in large areas of the church. Whether these negative results will finally outweigh the positive results of the campaigns remains to be seen—with the issue gravely in doubt.

V

The steadier we study this parable, the clearer the central point becomes: God expects us to cultivate the qualities of sensitivity and compassion in our attitudes and dealings with all men. Albert Schweitzer in his autobiography tells how God laid claim to him through this very parable. As he brooded over it, there came to him with unmistakable clarity and overwhelming power, the realization that Africa was the sick beggar at the door of Europe. Seeing this, he took the tack in life that established the mission and hospital at Lambaréné, and centered the attention of the Christian world on what can be done in a Christian way and by Christian means in the heart of Africa.

To put the parable negatively: It is a fearful thing to go through life blinded by self-love; to have eyes and see not, ears and hear not, a heart and feel no compassion for those in need; to have the ability to help but lack the compassion to do it.

It is a fearful thing so to insulate our Christian conscience in rationalizations that we are seldom moved to deeds of real love and compassion for others. And I suppose the most fearful thing of all is to be in a state of mind where we measure out our compassion crumb by crumb with no thought of self-giving or loving to the uttermost as God loves us.

To put it positively: the road to Christian maturity lies in the subordination of self to others, in losing oneself for the Gospel's sake. As Dr. Gregory Vlastos of Princeton University has well said, "To give one's life away to what one knows to be of highest worth, not only for oneself, but for all mankind is the most mature experience open to man."

The church is never more the Christian Church than when she sets before us opportunities for exhibiting and expressing in concrete terms our compassion for others. Christian compassion is not a word; it is a relationship between man and man and between the two persons involved and the God who loves them both. *When we help others, we serve God. And there is no other way of serving God than through humble obedience to His will in the service of human need.*

The light of God is falling
   Upon life's common way;
The master's voice still calling,
   "Come, walk with Me today."

No duty can seem lowly
   To him who lives with Thee,
And all of life grows holy,
   O Christ of Galilee![2]

10. How Blind Can We Be?

MATTHEW 21:33-41, 45-46

I

What we so easily call "the moment of truth" comes when man must accept the fact of failure, defeat, and perhaps of ultimate frustration in life. Our Lord is called upon to face this at the end of his life when he must accept the bitter fact that he can neither win the support of the scribes and the Pharisees nor longer evade their vengeance. So far from being intimidated by the prospect, he tells them plainly that God will turn their little victory into a great defeat and will give him the final triumph. He gives them this message in the parable of the wicked tenants, the meaning of which can be summed up in a single question: "How blind can men be?"

The parable tells of a hard-working, thrifty small farmer who had built a prosperous vineyard. He did this as a result of long-time strenuous work; he planned and planted it; he nurtured the vines to the stage of good production; he even built a watchtower from which to guard it against grazing animals and malicious men.

When business called him to a far country, he turned the care of the vineyard over to tenants. Doubtless he selected them with care. The understanding between them was clear: They were to pay him and to be paid themselves in produce—the usual form of rental payment. When it came time to collect and market his share of the crop—undoubtedly the larger share of it—he sent servants to take care of the operation.

But in the interval between the owner's departure and servants' return, something had happened to—rather in—the hearts of the tenants. While we have no way of knowing exactly what it was, I do not think we are far afield if we think of the tenants' reasoning in some such fashion as this: "We have worked the soil, cared for the crop, kept watch over it night and day. Without us there would be no crop at all. By rights, the crop is ours. The owner had no part in this. Why should he get any of it, let alone the lion's share of it?"

Or they may have reasoned, "Why should we pay him? He is too far away to do anything about it if we should refuse. Several years may pass before he can return to make trouble for us. During that time, we can market the entire crop and hide the money. If he does have us evicted, we will have the money and can get another job somewhere. What have we to lose?"

While we must speculate on how they rationalized it, we do not need to speculate on what they did. They drove his servants away with increasing ferocity—beating one, stoning another, and finally killing one.

The owner sent a second group of servants who met the same fate. Then he made a serious miscalculation in the workings of human nature. He knew how much he loved his son. He thought the tenants loved him, too. He may have recalled how they played with the boy while he was yet at home in the vineyard. So he reasoned, "They will respect my son," and sent him.

When the tenants saw him coming, their greed leaped into the driver's seat and drove them over the precipice. They did not love and respect him, saying: "This is his son." Rather in greed and malice they said, "This is his heir." So they killed him, hoping thereby either to intimidate the owner or, at least, to buy more time in which to line their pockets.

Jesus asked his listeners, "What will the owner do to those tenants when he comes?" and got the answer, "He will put those wretches to a miserable death and let out the vineyards to other tenants who will give him the fruits in their season."

II

The importance of the story grows on us when we see what it meant when first spoken and what it meant later in the church.

Looking squarely at the scribes and the Pharisees to whom the parable was told Jesus said, in effect, "You are planning to kill me and are able to do so, but God will right the wrong which you commit in your blindness and sin."

The early church treasured the story for three reasons: (1) it helped explain the rejection and crucifixion of Jesus by the Jews; (2) it explained the destruction of Jerusalem by the Romans in A.D. 70; and (3) it gave them a clue to the importance of their role in the kingdom of God. They felt themselves to be the new tenants of God's vineyard, the new chosen people to whom God had entrusted His precious word and gospel.

We do not need to read more than a half-dozen pages in the earliest history we have of the early church—the book of Acts—to realize how much the first preachers depended on this line of reasoning. God had entrusted the nurture of His vineyard to the Chosen People, Israel. But they refused to honor His agreement with them. They would neither worship Him nor keep His commandments. They stoned and killed the prophets He sent with warnings. Finally, He sent His Son, thinking he would be respected. But they killed him. "Therefore," cried the early Christian preachers, "God has punished the wretches who did this; He has turned over the nurture of His kingdom to those who will respect and adore His Son."

Important as it is for us to see how this parable fits into the life and work of the early church, we must not forget that its permanent appeal comes from a quite different quarter. It has lived because of what it tells all men about themselves. What a pitiless light it throws on us—on our blindness to God's love and justice!

III

How blind can we be to what God gives us? The vineyard of this earth in which we labor was prepared by God and entrusted to us by Him. It is good doctrine—whether stated simply or abstractly—that God is the Creator of this universe, of this earth, and of life. We discover that we have a good life, a good earth, and a friendly or, at least, a Spirit- and purpose-centered universe. All these things—and many more beyond our imagining—God entrusts to us for our care, our use, our enjoyment, and our fulfillment.

What a privileged form of life we are! Endowed of God with mind, heart, body, will, and conscience; blessed by the need for both man and God, and given every opportunity to find and know both, we do not roll about like insensible billiard balls on a cosmic table at the impulse of blind, unfeeling forces outside us. We are *human beings,* made in the image of God; capable of love, understanding, sympathy, and sharing. We are so created as to be able to know each other and, miracle of miracles, to know God, too. Who will attempt to measure the worth of so great a gift as a life like ours in a world like this with people like those around us, and with the privilege of humble fellowship with the Creator of all? How can we help crying, "Holy, holy, holy is the Lord of Hosts. The whole earth is full of His glory." Yet who of us will not confess that we plod through day after day blind to the glory of it all?

We are blind, too, to the responsibilities of life. For life is not all rejoicing in such glory—in fact, its true glory is found in the hard, creative work given us to do.

It is a major musical tragedy that Maltbie D. Babcock's fine poem, "Be Strong!" has been entombed in an unsingable tune—but, tune or no, the truth of the poem is undeniable:

> We are not here to play, to dream, to drift;
> We have hard work to do, and loads to lift.
> Shun not the struggle, face it, 'tis God's gift.
> It matters not how deep entrenched the wrong,
> How hard the battle goes, the day, how long;
> Faint not, fight on! To-morrow comes the song.[1]

Life is ennobled, enriched, and made livable by hard work, by the acceptance and assumption of exacting responsibilities that stretch every energy we have to the breaking point. Truly great lives are always reaching out for something more to do—and they are made radiant by the effort.

But for every Jane Addams who sees and is made radiant by the moral earnestness of life, there are ten thousand of us who are blind to it. Edna Ferber must have had Jane Addams in mind when she wrote, "Some people make the world; the rest of us just come along and live in it." A life that is blind to our responsibilities to each other and to God; a life that is given to self-centeredness, self-concern, and self-pity is no fit life for one who is a child of God and who is called to be a coworker with God in the building of a kingdom of love.

Not all our blindness is due to malice and premeditated plans to hurt others. Sometimes I think only the small part of the anguish of the world springs from that kind of intentional blindness. More, much more, springs from the sort of blindness Edward Rowland Sill describes in his poem, "The Fool's Prayer."

'Tis not by guilt the onward sweep
 Of truth and right, O Lord, we stay;
'Tis by our follies that so long
 We hold the earth from heaven away.

These clumsy feet, still in the mire,
 Go crushing blossoms without end;
These hard well-meaning hands we thrust
 Among the heart-strings of a friend.

The ill-timed truth we might have kept—
 Who knows how sharp it pierced and stung?
The word we had not sense to say—
 Who knows how grandly it had rung?

Our faults no tenderness should ask,
 The chastening stripes must cleanse them all;
But for our blunders—oh, in shame
 Before the eyes of heaven we fall.[2]

Can anyone say he does not know what the poet is talking about? I cannot, and I doubt whether many men will even pretend innocence. Times without number, we have thrust "these hard, well-meaning hands" of ours "among the heart-strings of a friend."

In blindness, not malice or premeditated evil, we have done it. And, as frequently as not, our blindness springs from a limited vision of what we think ought to be done. Wanting it, believing in it, we become insensitive to what our proposal means to others, and we hurt them almost beyond healing.

I do not suppose it is possible to keep from ever hurting each other through blindness, but I am sure we could get along with a lot less of it than we now have. And we would, too, if we were honestly to ask of any proposition which we back, "How will this affect this person, or that one, or another?" The most important fact in any proposal is the human equation. Even when such hurt is unavoidable, it can be lessened by the kind of sensitivity and understanding that any one of us can learn and have.

The last week in the life of our Lord is the crowning example of the blindness rather than the malice of men like ourselves. To be sure, the religious leaders of Jesus' day knew what they were about and pursued their course with cruel deliberation. But everyone else had been blinded by one thing or another—and in the end an innocent man was murdered.

IV

If you ask what blinds us to the glory of God and to the moral earnestness of life, our religious tradition gives us the answer in one hard word: *Sin!*

There is no point wasting time playing tricks with theological doctrines about the idea of sin. It means, basically, a conscious violation of the known will of God. It calls attention to the fact that man—all men—must fight against and overcome a deep and universal unwillingness to hear and to obey God. We find it easier and more pleasant to obey ourselves, or someone else, or the state—anything or anyone short of God. But the logic of our faith hammers home the hard point that obedience to anyone other than God is a sin that blinds the human spirit.

There is, unfortunately, nothing abstract about it. And as Anselm once warned, "We must not underestimate the gravity of sin." Sin as the conscious violation of the known will of God will blind—indeed, does blind—us to the true relationships we ought to have with each other and with God. The churchmen of the Middle Ages did not shrink from listing what they called "the seven deadly sins." And they are as deadly today as ever. Pride, covetousness, lust, anger, gluttony, envy, slothfulness—let any of them get control of us and we are blind indeed. Go over the list—better, go over our lives in the light of the list—and we will never doubt the power of sin to blind us. One of the great old prayers of the church strikes deep roots in our own experiences:

Forgive us, O Lord, the sins of our youth and our age, the sins of our soul and the sins of our body, our secret sins, our presumptuous and crying sins, the sins we have done to please ourselves and the sins we have done to please others. Forgive those sins which we know, and those sins which we do not know because of our sin against thy Holy Spirit. May the same Spirit convict us of those sins which we have never dared to acknowledge even to ourselves, as of those sins which have so laid hold upon us that we no longer confess them to be sins.[3]

V

The church finds herself crippled today by the blindness of men. Sometimes it is the blindness of men outside the church to the purpose of the church. Sometimes it is the blindness of those of us in the church to the message and mission of the church.

When men regard the church as one among many social institutions, they are blind to what makes the church the church. For the church is not a social organization at all. It is a congregation of those who have heard God's word in Christ and who are drawn into fellowship with others who have had a similar experience. The fellowship we have with each other in the church is but the beginning—the first step, as it were—of our response to that word of love we hear in Jesus Christ. Under the continual prompting and guidance of that word, we are called to be creative instruments in the building of the kingdom of God in the lives of men. We are called of God in Christ to proclaim the reality of the kingdom of love and to bring ourselves and our day under the judgment of it.

This claim must sound complicated, if not arrogant, to one who has not been nurtured in the church—and possibly to some who have been in the church all their lives. But it does underscore the all-important fact about the church.

The church owes her primary loyalty to the word of God as we hear it in Christ; no state, no society, no way of life can expect the church to treat it as God. The church tries to be the conscious servant of Him before whom the kings and kingdoms of this earth must stand for judgment.

When we become a member of the church, we do not surrender our citizenship in this country, but we do agree to subordinate that citizenship to our call to serve the kingdom of God as we find it in Jesus Christ. We are to be in the world but not of the world. We are to resist the efforts of the world to mold our faith and to persist in the effort to mold the world by our faith.

So long as we miss that fact about the church, we shall be blind to her mission and message. We shall misunderstand what she does and the spirit in which she goes about it. I can understand how people outside the church might be blind to all this, but it is hard to see how so many in the church have missed it.

We are so like the wicked tenants in Jesus' parable. We treat the church as though she belongs to us. We will work for her, care for her, but only on the assumption that she is ours and will say what we want her to say, will do what we want her to do. And when the call comes to pay our supreme loyalty to the God who called the church into being, we plot how we can escape doing it. Though He sends us prophetic spirits to strike the blinders from our eyes, we drive them out, thinking to be rid of their troublesome notions. And, in the end, we discover that we have slain the Spirit of the Son Himself rather than be led by Him in high paths of loyalty to God.

We have no greater need, no more pressing duty, in the church today than the revitalizing of our loyalty to the One whose name we bear. For the blind cannot lead the blind.

11. The Word and the Deed

LUKE 7:18-35

I

I hope Abraham Lincoln will forgive us this paraphrase of one of his best-known lines: "You can please some of the people all of the time and all of the people some of the time, but you can't please all of the people all of the time." And the fickle character of public approval even when you have it has come up for grim notice repeatedly by thoughtful writers. Plato for example gives up on democracy because he is sure that the mob will be given to villainy and then to tyranny. Machiavelli is so convinced of the undependable nature of ordinary men that he thinks democracy a lost cause and turns to a benevolent but firm monarchy as the only dependable form of government.

Jesus is giving his own unique reaction to the dependability of the crowd when he confronts a very select company of scribes and Pharisees who gathered around him as they had around John the Baptist. They were comparing the two prophetic leaders. Jesus had heard their complaints about John and now their complaints about him. "John was too stern, too grim, too aloof, too hopeless. You are too joyful, too approachable, too much of a mixer with everyone who wants to see you. John fasted; you feast. John mourned over the Day of the Lord; you rejoice over the coming of the kingdom of God."

So the comments went among the people and their learned leaders. Jesus saw at once that they were dodging the main issue in what he was saying, even as they had evaded the main point in the preaching of John.

Instead of facing up to the fact of God's judgment on them and their wickedness, they were devoting themselves to the little things

THE WORD AND THE DEED

about Jesus and John that they somehow did not like. They were trying
to give Jesus and John what we would call the "brush-off"—and they
were succeeding to their own satisfaction.

Jesus said to them, whether in irony or humor we are not able to
say, "You remind me of children who say you want to play games,
yet who don't want to play any game that is suggested. Should someone
say, 'Let us pretend to be in a funeral procession and wail and chant
dirges,' you say, 'No; it's too sad, too depressing.' But should someone
suggest, 'Let's play at being at a wedding and sing and dance with joy,
you say, 'No, it's too happy, too cheerful' " Jesus was saying, in effect,
"You are wise men, undoubtedly, and your wisdom will bear fruit even
though you are behaving now like captious children."

We may be sure his hearers neither liked nor missed the point of
his parable. But there is no evidence at all that they changed their
habit of dwelling on, and carping over, details and dodging the main
issues. Jesus rightly charged them with casuistry and open insincerity
in evading the purpose of God to which he and John were bearing
witness. He called for earnestness, integrity, and honesty in facing this
purpose and *he opened his public ministry by sounding the most unwelcome note ever to fall on human ears: the note of judgment—"Repent! The kingdom is at hand!"*

Jesus picked up the note of judgment which he heard from the
trumpet of John and sounded it with great firmness. But the ones who
heard refused to take it seriously. Both John and Jesus tried to force
their generation to face themselves in the light of God's will, to see
and acknowledge their spiritual poverty, superficiality, and complacency.
They called for deeds not words, deeds of penitence, deeds of obedience,
deeds becoming one who was a citizen of God's kingdom.

Jesus was not the first to be and to know that the heart of his message was being dodged by people who simply refused to face what he
was saying. The prophets before him had gone through the same thing
time and again. It is still heartbreaking to read their pleas for a hearing,
to see them treated as objects of curiosity, ridicule, anger or simply
ignored by their generation. And though the children of the ones who
so treated them were to revere them and hail them as God's chosen
leaders, the prophets in the later generation fared no better than their
predecessors.

In fact the later prophets would appeal to their generation in the names of the now revered earlier prophets—but the same cycle repeated itself relentlessly. The people paid no attention to what they were saying. And we see the same cycle repeating itself in the experience of Jesus.

John's protest, except as it was caught up and conserved in Jesus, seems to have gone begging completely. Although he was the center of a good deal of contagion for awhile, there were practically no carryovers in terms of any sort of influence on social institutions or the life of people. While most of John's hearers did drift away from him, a few hung on for several generations and then slipped into oblivion.

It looked as though the same thing were going to happen to Jesus. While most of his hearers turned away from him, his life and works found effective lodgment in the fellowship of his disciples who became the center of the Christian Church. And although this fellowship was very small for a long time, it grew rapidly and became the carrier of the legitimate protest and note of judgment sounded by both John and Jesus. The Christian Church has continued to be a fellowship whose primary task was and must be to preach the gospel of judgment, salvation, and love, for God's sake. That is as truly our task today as ever it has been the task of churchmen before us.

II

The Christian Church is on the march today with a vigor and purpose seldom equaled or surpassed in her long and checkered career. From one end of the world to the other, she is astir and on the move. Like Wordsworth's Happy Warrior, she knows and rejoices in the fact that great issues are being joined not alone in these days but also in her very life. Yet her happiness is far from simple bubbling joy. The issues are tremendous in scope and depth and utterly tragic in their import. They encompass the whole range of our life, and the fate of what we call civilization is clearly hanging in the balances.

The church is facing up to this fact, aware of her guilt in its existence and painfully conscious of her unworthiness to deal with it, yet solemnly committed to the same message that Jesus and John brought to their generation, namely, the message of the judgment of God on us and our generation.

This is the motif of the mighty efforts toward co-operation among the churches in the National and World Councils of Churches. We know that the effective pronunciation of this message depends upon our unity. We stand together or fall separately. If we speak with one voice on this matter, we have a chance of being heard; if we speak separately, no one will pay attention to us. We know that the issues which unite us as churches are more important than the ones which divide us.

We know that the foes we face are faced by all of us, not just by some of us. We believe that through our togetherness we can sound a note of judgment in our generation with such seriousness that it will be heard and can exalt a high moral and spiritual purpose in our common life that may lead us out of the wastelands of endless compromises, ambiguous moralities, and pseudo religions that now threaten us in every quarter.

Wherever churchmen get together there is agreement on the one overarching duty of the church today: *Preach the gospel.* That is the unbroken witness of every Ecumenical Conference over the last thirty years. That was and continues to be the assumption on which church conferences proceed as they wrestle with the economic, social, racial, and international issues of our time. The great cry of the Third Assembly of the World Council in New Delhi was to stop talking about structure and organization and to begin talking seriously about mission, the evangelization of the world. We are supposed to preach the gospel, not study the intricacies of the ecclesiastical structure!

This sort of an experience is what one would expect today. Every generation of Christians for nearly two thousand years has been forced even as we are now to consider the meaning of the gospel for our life and time. Sometimes the forcing agent has been a powerful personality, like Paul, Luther, or Wesley, who through the sheer power of his insight, conviction, and life was able to bring his contemporaries to a new awareness of the reality of the gospel. Other times, the forcing agent has been the obvious contradiction between the gospel we have inherited and the nature of the world in which we live. A man must be dull beyond all hope if he is not pierced to the quick by such contradictions in our world today. Consider a few of them.

The gospel preaches peace; the world is in a state of war, cold or hot. The gospel preaches justice; the world-ferment roots in injustices of every sort. The gospel proclaims love; the world seethes with hatred. The gospel urges forgiveness and love of enemy; the world has brought the rationalization, the art and the facilities of vengeance and retaliation to a level of appalling efficiency. The gospel urges men to seek first the kingdom of God, finding thereby peace of mind and spirit as well as true security; the world is seeking security by building up situations of strength, by treaties, by the accumulation of weapons of all sorts, and by creating in the minds and spirits of men a will to war.

Given these glaring contradictions between the gospel and the world today, we who believe in the gospel, yet live in this world, have our work cut out for us. The worst mistake we could make, I suppose, would be to play down the seriousness of the contradictions, hoping thereby to reduce the tensions and the possible tragedy of our witness to the gospel. Equally serious, in my judgment, would be to wait, like Festus, for a more convenient season in which to push the claims of the gospel. Still another mistake would be for us to believe or assume or encourage others to believe that we who are trying to proclaim the gospel possess, in detail, the needed answers to every great problem faced by men today. That, patently, is untrue, and we must be the first to admit it even as we insist that the gospel contains the answer we seek.

I am sure there will be agreement among us on the observation that we are playing for the stakes of life and death for our civilization as we proclaim the gospel today. It may easily be either life or death for the human race on the face of this planet. Yet the gospel we have inherited is adequate even to issues like these. We who proclaim it do so not because of our wisdom or spiritual worthiness but because we believe it, and believe it to be the way to life, and believe that it contains the sheer strength we need to walk in that way. This gospel that I am speaking about begins with us, as it did in Jesus' day, with the most unwelcome note ever to fall on human ears: the note of judgment. There is no other place at which the Christian gospel can begin. The call today is as it was in the first century: "Repent ye, the kingdom is at hand."

III

So far as I can see the gospel required us to make four closely related statements about the nature and the meaning of this judgment we are proclaiming: (1) God alone is Judge of all the earth; (2) the judgment of God is incarnate in Jesus Christ; (3) that judgment still stands; (4) we are the custodians of it.

Of course the idea that God is the Judge of all the earth is much older than Christianity. The Hebrews had discovered it the hard way over several hundred years of history before it was articulated in the New Testament. The prophets had given it pungent expression and made it a power in Hebrew life and thought. Some of its most powerful interpretations are to be found in their writings. Since Jesus and his disciples were all Jews, they had been nurtured in this tradition and accepted it without question.

The idea of judgment has played a prominent part in the Christian gospel from the day when Jesus began his public ministry. Strictly speaking, the Christian era began when Jesus brought his contemporaries under that sweeping judgment: "Repent, for the kingdom of heaven is at hand." Here was the announcement of something new; something for which men could and must prepare. They were called to repent and whatever else repentance may mean, it does mean that a judgment has been passed on the life of a person or a people. It means that they have been weighed and found wanting by God himself. It means that a serious and far-reaching redirection of life must be made at once.

Legend has it that Clovis, wild king of the Franks, halted his baptism into the Christian faith long enough to ask the missionary, Remigius, what this new way of life would mean. Remigius answered, "Adore what you used to burn, and burn what you used to adore." That was plain enough for Clovis and much too plain for most of us. Although the spirit of this advice is quite out of step with the spirit of compromise in so much of our thought and life, it is surely in keeping with the entire emphasis in New Testament times. For the early preachers did not attempt to play down the radical nature of the gospel, lest men be offended. Rather they sounded it forth loud and clear that men might be saved from their sins. When the trembling jailer asked Paul what he had to do to be saved, Paul had an answer that demanded the complete reorientation of the life of the jailer and his family.

This emphasis upon the reality of judgment runs like an unbroken thread through the New Testament. It is so apparent in the Gospel of Matthew that that book has sometimes been called "the Gospel of Judgment." Matthew, more than the other Gospels, presents Jesus as the judge of men, bringing upon them and their works the voice and spirit of God's judgment. He records the ringing judgments upon the hypocritical scribes and Pharisees. He tells how Jesus sent would-be disciples away with these stinging words, "No man having put his hand to the plow and looking back is fit for the kingdom of God." Matthew alone dwells on Jesus' judgment and lament over Jerusalem as the city that killed the prophets and which, in turn, must be destroyed.

Jesus was always exposing this process of judgment to his hearers. The rich young ruler wanted eternal life, and it is clear that he could have qualified if he chose wisely. But when he saw what was involved, he turned away. There is a sense in which he passed judgment upon himself by refusing to follow Jesus' advice, but I doubt whether that will do justice to Jesus' thought on the matter. So far as we can determine, his mind went along some such lines as these: God had set before this young man various courses of conduct. Among them he not only could choose, he had to choose—and he had to live with the consequences of his choice. In a very real sense, then, God is the creator of the alternatives before men and the determiner of the consequences which follow from them all. But He leaves to man the freedom to choose, requiring of him simply and fairly that once he has walked through the door of one alternative he be prepared to live with the consequences of that choice. It is Jesus' firm faith that God's will toward man is best described as the love of a father for his son; that the alternatives before man are not creations of malice but of a sincere desire to make it possible for men to live as true sons of God.

This, better than anything else, describes the judgment which Jesus passed on his generation—the judgment his hearers were passing by so lightly. He set their ideas and institutions, their conventions and convictions, their ordinary daily habits and their religious customs against the backdrop of eternity. There is nothing vague or abstract about the way he did it, if we follow the Gospel story. He made loyalty to him the test of loyalty to the will of God. He was convinced that the kingdom of God was at hand; and he was convinced that he knew how God wanted men to live if they would enter that kingdom. That was his call to preach—the force that lifted him out of the carpenter's shop and set him on the highways of his homeland. He outlined his faith over and over again, demanding that men choose for or against him, warning them that everything hinged on that choice. He asked them to leave all and follow him. He warned them that he was but articulating the choice he discovered in the very nature of the world and life as created by, and answerable to, God. He assured them that God wanted them to choose the kind of life that would lead to transforming fellowship with Him and with each other.

The greatest painter with the greatest theme ever to burst on the vision of man, he sketched the love of God for man, the possibility of a life lost in God, in firm line and bold color. He knew what he wanted to say and he said it with all the power and authority of his life. His presentations have never been equaled; they pierce us to the core of our compromises and half truths; they open up doors that no man can close, but through which no man can force us to walk. He underscored his teachings with his life, and he called upon his disciples to do likewise, no matter what the cost.

IV

You know the result. Most people treated him as a fanatic or misguided young idealist, or simply laughed at him. They turned away from him and his impossible notions, undoubtedly comforting one another with the sage advice, "You have to be realistic." But even as the overwhelming majority turned away, a few remained, not quite sure of the wisdom of their choice. But when he asked, "Will you too go away?" they made answer, "Lord, to whom shall we go? Thou hast the words of eternal life."

In their thought, in their preaching, in the books that they wrote or influenced, in the church they gave their lives to build, Jesus Christ became the incarnation of the continuing judgment of God on the lives of men, the judgment we receive and articulate in our life and times.

It is the contention of the Christian faith that that evaluation of Jesus Christ is correct. It is our deepest conviction that that judgment still stands at the center of life and history. That is what Christian theologians mean when they say that the cross stands at the center of life and history. He continues to be a decisive fact in life because he requires a decision of us. Like Augustine, we may put it off for years, but all the time we know we are missing something of transcendent importance about this business of living. We may not like the choices he asks us to make. They are hard ones; so hard we want someone else to make the first break.

It remains for Lin Yutang, in his book *Between Tears and Laughter* to sharpen up one of the choices that hurts the most today: "Peace on earth, . . . is an act of faith, and without faith we shall not be saved. It boils down almost to this: Jesus, the Prince of Peace, was a liar or He was not. We've got to make up our minds."[1] And, I should like to add, we must be prepared to redesign our lives, refashion our attitudes, and share in the transformation of every institution that keeps the clear witness of his glory from breaking through into radiant expression. We shall be utterly unworthy of him if we accept casually the brush-off which we are receiving as a church even as he received it in his life and time. Let us bear our witness without fear or favor, confident of our calling and rejoicing in the fact that we have been called of God to be witnesses to His love as we see it in Jesus Christ.

12. The Power to Receive Great Things

I

Thomas R. Kelly, a gifted American writer and teacher, is credited with this sobering description of all too many of us in all too many of our moods: "We expect great things with no real power to receive them." Jesus of Nazareth long ago discovered this lamentable trait of human beings and gave it immortal expression in his parable of the sower.

Scholars are agreed that this parable signifies one of the turning points in Jesus' life and ministry. He was doing what every man must do sooner or later: Make a realistic appraisal of the success of his work. His public ministry had been underway for some considerable time, and it had seemed to be a great success. At least, the crowds came by the thousands to hear him preach. At times crowd emotions mounted to the peak of near hysteria as they proclaimed him the Messiah.

His disciples were beside themselves with joy and eager expectation: Perhaps the kingdom was actually at hand! Perhaps they were living in the last days! Each time they saw the multitudes pressing in upon Jesus their hearts beat faster. They had failed to notice one thing that Jesus had not missed: Many came, but few stayed. Thousands would wait around for a miracle, especially if it might benefit them, but they melted away when the Great Teacher started to talk about putting first things first, about subordinating physical and material concerns to spiritual matters, about sacrifice to the point of losing their life for the sake of the kingdom.

Seeing this fact and correctly appraising its significance, Jesus took his disciples to one side and related the now famous parable of the sower. Perhaps it should be called the parable of the soils, as some suggest,

97

since it centers attention on the various kinds of soil on which the seeds fall. Call it what we will, the main point is the same. Jesus was saying in effect, "I have been preaching the kingdom of God to all. Although thousands have heard it, let us not be deceived about their response. Only a few are actually taking it to heart. The rest, he said, "will believe for awhile, and then they will forget all about it." He draws a sharp contrast between two types of people: (1) those who hearing, believe for awhile, then turn away; (2) "those who, hearing the word, hold it fast in an honest and good heart, and bring forth fruit with patience."

Fragmentary though our Gospel records are, they support this analysis of the crowds that surrounded Jesus of Nazareth. Wherever he turned, he encountered a multitude who, to use Kelly's phrase, expected great things with no real power to receive them.

There were those who toyed with the notion of becoming disciples. They felt his greatness; they sensed the overpowering wonder of the kingdom which he preached—but they sensed this from afar. They sensed it as a traveler in the mountains hears a mighty thunderstorm muttering among distant peaks. Having heard it, he makes for cover with all possible speed. It is quite different to hear a storm in a distance and to be enveloped in it.

These would-be disciples of Jesus wanted him to give them something great—whereas he was inviting them to prepare themselves for the great event of letting God have full possession of their lives. "Too hard," said some. "Too long," said others; "we want something right now." "Too fanciful," said still others; "we do not want to become dealers in dreams; we want to live by fact."

Even his disciples wanted, expected, and planned early tangible benefits of his greatness—only to discover that they had no real power to receive them, let alone share them. Recall, if you will, the incident of the epileptic boy at the foot of the Mount of Transfiguration. The disciples had failed to heal him, and after Jesus succeeded, they asked, "Why could we not do that?" Jesus answered, in effect, "This kind of healing is accomplished by nothing save prayer." That must have stung them because they, like us, were better at sleeping than at praying.

They expected great things but had no real power to receive them. That, I repeat, is a custom-made description of most people who heard Jesus of Nazareth then or who have heard the Christian gospel over the ensuing centuries. We draw close to him; we glimpse from afar the great realities he speaks of; we may even believe for awhile; but only a few will hold his word fast "in an honest and good heart, and bring forth fruit with patience."

II

This problem of expecting great things with no real power to receive them misses no one. We face it wherever we turn, and we will face it as long as we live. Whether we are student or professor, minister or layman, professional person or homemaker, we would do well to accept it as one of the most urgent spiritual problems of our lives.

One thing is clear: We do not get great things either by expecting or wanting them alone. The "gimme" attitude toward life is all wrong. It is a complete misreading of the human situation. There is a widely prevalent philosophy of life, though not often articulated in just these words, that the world owes us a living. A wise psychiatrist once defined a neurotic person as one who thinks the world owes him a "loving." Actually, the world owes us nothing that it does not pay day in and day out. It is we who owe the world—and we try to twist and squirm out of the obligation as best we can. The world owes us neither a living nor a loving, but it provides us with the opportunities to earn both if we want them and are willing to share in them.

We want, need, and confidently expect that somehow or other we are going to get great things. Students want a good education and a sound professional training. All of us want a well-rounded, well-poised personality. We want to achieve stable, creative relationships with friends in our homes and with our colleagues. We want to live in a peaceful world. In our more reflective moments we might even confess that we want to be at peace with ourselves, with other men, and with God.

These are great and good expectations, hopes, and ideals. But, all the wanting, all the needing, and all the expecting in the world will not ensure their delivery in our lives. All are possible of achievement; none lies beyond our reach, placed there by immutable decree. Yet no one can give them to us on order or on request. We will yearn for them, even weep for them, perhaps even pray for them—but will we prepare ourselves to receive them?

Thomas Kelly did. In his first encounter with Rufus Jones, at Haverford College, he said: "I am just going to make my life a miracle!"[1] And he did in a strangely human and humble way. Not the kind of miracle that would arrest the attention of people who want to gape in stupid credulity at what they are told on solemn authority are the highly irregular antics of the sun in the sky. But his life was the kind of miracle you can live with, believe in, and take as daily bread for your spirit. Kelly not only expected great things, but he spent his brief life cultivating the power to receive them.

He was a conscientious and gifted student. Loving the routine of academic life, he was so sensitive to the needs of others that he twice interrupted his career as student and teacher to serve with the American Friends Service Committee in overseas service. He became an inspiring teacher—one who made each student feel that his life could and should be a miracle. His writings speak eloquently of the fact that his spiritual growth reached that point where he could receive the crowning gift of life: He walked daily with God.

His preparation for great things yielded a vision of purpose in life, the courage to try to translate it into fact, the strength to recover from inevitable defeat, poise in life, and peace in the presence of death.

You ask why we are loathe to do this, and for answer I invite you to come with me to the Art Institute of Chicago and stand before the statue which interprets in marble Victor Hugo's famous lines: "I feel two natures struggling within me." There are two figures composing this statue: one, the ideal nature, the other the base nature of life. The ideal nature symbolizes every good, creative impulse, desire, and aspiration of man. Softness of line, warmth of expression, and simple radiance characterize this figure which stands almost erect, face lifted toward the things that ought to be. The other figure, base nature, is utterly different. It symbolizes the evil, destructive, selfish forces forever at work in life and in the world: pride, greed, lust, anger, fear, envy—all these have left their mark in the brutal, coarse, almost bestial features of this figure which lies sprawled at the feet of the one symbolizing ideal nature, yet clings inseparably to it.

As we study this work of art, we have our answer to why we are loathe to prepare ourselves to receive great things. The power to receive great things depends upon our ability to conquer the enemies of greatness that inhabit, like so many demons, the soul of every man. George Meredith once put it in these lines from *Modern Love*:

> In tragic life, God wot,
> No villain need be! Passions spin the plot:
> We are betrayed by what is false within.

No one knew better than Jesus Christ what these enemies of great-ness are. He singles them out with almost pitiless clarity in his Sermon on the Mount, and he identifies them as the "false within" which betrays us. How well we know them all!

Fear is one such enemy: fear for tomorrow; fear of the unknown; fear of new experiences.

Love of the wrong things is another enemy: Material possessions, things near at hand; love of those things that give us security, power, recognition among men; desire for things, for wealth, for a good name among men; a willingness to exploit the person of another for our own satisfaction, which is lust; a willingness to exploit the possessions of an-other for our own satisfaction, which is greed.

Hatred is another enemy: Cursing another until our life is a spreading pool of bitterness; seeking the destruction of another; a willingness even to vault to the judgment throne of God himself and usurp his ultimate prerogative, passing judgments of life and death on others.

What a shambles these enemies can make of our life—and will make unless we can learn how to overcome them. Jesus' recommendation is simple and still holds: Put first things first; love and trust God utterly; and seek his kingdom as you move into the future.

III

Once in a while a student goes to college and seminary in the "gimme" frame of mind. He thinks that getting an education is like that magic moment in a New Year's party when at the appointed time someone pulls a string and enough balloons float down for each merry-maker to have one. A school does not owe a student an education. It owes him only the right to get an education if he is willing to prepare himself to receive one—which is a quite different matter. A school owes him a good library and a good faculty, but even these cannot give him anything he is not willing to receive. A cynic may define a lecture as the process by which an idea passes from the mind of the professor to the mind of the student without visible effort by, or effect on, either one. But the student will soon find out that this is not true. A high serious-ness as well as hard work pervades all good instruction and learning. When he steps into a great university library, there will be a hundred thousand voices trying to tell him things, but he must have ears to hear before they can get anything at all across to him. He must be prepared to receive their instruction, or they are powerless to help. He will find that the wisest teachers will not be the ones who try to give him something, but the ones who encourage, strengthen, and promise to accompany him on his own search for understanding. Every student has a right to expect great things, but under God he must prepare himself to receive them.

Frequently couples will enter marriage expecting to receive a stable, creative, joyful home without realizing that they must earn the power to receive it. They must learn how to live as responsible participants in a shared relationship. They must constantly cultivate an ever deepening sensitivity to each other. They must be aware of and willing to accept the discipline of marriage and the home. They must be willing to lose themselves in the process of homemaking if they would win the kind of home they expect, and have a right to expect.

This is a vastly different picture of a home from the one that shines through the biting verse by Elise Peckham:

> The marriage lasted twenty years;
> They followed separate careers.
> Lately they parted, without regret;
> Unaware they had never met.[2]

We expect freedom, we say—freedom as a person and freedom as a people. We have said it so long and so loud of late that it now carries the overtones of hysteria. We have even gone to the extent of trying to divide the world into two parts: slave and free. Of course the debate rages over where the line of demarcation runs, but we blandly assume that there is one, and that we are on the right side of it. That is bad enough, but it is not the whole story. We insist or suspect that when anyone disagrees with us on major matters he is on the other side of the line even though he may be our next-door neighbor!

Let me make just two observations about this large matter, observations that relate it directly to the theme we are considering: (1) I am certain that it is quite impossible to throw the nations of the world into two categories—slave and free; (2) I am equally certain that there is a vast difference between those who believe in the spirit of liberty as suggested by Justice Learned Hand and those who do not. Hear again a few lines from Justice Hand's now famous address;

What then is the spirit of liberty? I cannot define it; I can only tell you my own faith. The spirit of liberty is the spirit which is not too sure that it is right; the spirit of liberty is the spirit which seeks to understand the minds of other men and women; the spirit of liberty is the spirit which weighs their interests alongside its own without bias; the spirit of liberty remembers that not even a sparrow falls to earth unheeded; the spirit of liberty is the spirit of Him who, near two thousand years ago taught mankind that lesson it has never learned, but has never quite forgotten; that there may be a kingdom where the least shall be heard and considered side by side with the greatest.[3]

Can anyone honestly expect so great a gift as this spirit of liberty to come to us by the simple right of birth and citizenship in this or any other country? We either seek it with all our hearts or miss it completely. We need it badly, almost more than anything else, if our thrust for freedom for all men is to make either sense or progress. But the spirit of liberty is as far removed as anything could possibly be from the dogmatism, the arrogance, and the will to coerce people into conformity now plainly evident all over the world.

It is one thing to sing about freedom and to expect liberty to reign over us, and quite another to seek the power to receive so great a gift.

We expect world peace, we say; that is, we think we are entitled to it. We want it; we know we must have it; its achievement is the goal of all responsible statesmanship as well as the burden of every honest prayer. But have we the power to receive it—aye, there's the rub. This we know: It will not, it cannot be given to us by anyone at any time or for any one reason. We must make its achievement the central goal of our personal and common life and be willing to rethink, as need be, everything that separates us from others if we are to be ready to receive world peace.

T. S. Eliot in his play, *Murder in the Cathedral*, has Thomas À Becket say, "Death will come only when I am worthy of it."

We will get world peace when we are worthy of it—and not one day before. So great a gift will come only when we accept it as the most important fact of our time. This means we must recover from the fanatical determination to have a world cut to the pattern of our desires and are willing to take the rest of mankind into serious account; when we are willing to subordinate all life to the will of God as we see it in Christ; when we are willing to try to bring the relationships of races, nations, and cultures under the judgment of the One who made all men.

When we are prepared to receive world peace God will give it to us —and He cannot give it to us before we are ready to receive it. The proclamation of this hard but hopeful fact is the most urgent responsibility of the Church today. And I say "urgent" advisedly. Mankind has made the last mistake it can hope to survive. We may flinch from the alternative confronting us, but it is ours to face: either we will be the best generation morally and spiritually speaking that this old world has ever seen, or we will be the last one. We do well to tremble at the thought that God seems to have placed man's last chance to continue on the face of this earth with people like us. Since we dare act on no other assumption, let us then with full and firm faith in Him prepare ourselves to receive the gift of a genuine human family in which men will dwell in peace, justice, and brotherhood.

13. God's Ultimatum to Man

JOHN 15:1-11

I

We may not like the idea of an ultimatum, but we discover one wherever we turn in great religion. In fact we can devise a rough kind of formula: No ultimatum, no greatness of faith. For a great faith requires a firm commitment as a condition of creative participation in the fellowship of the faithful.

This was certainly true in the life and teachings of our Lord. When he wanted to stress the necessity of firm commitment as a condition of discipleship and service in his kingdom, he did so not alone by direct invitation but by the use of parables that make the point with utmost clarity. One of the best known of these is in the Gospel of John and begins with the words: "I am the true vine, and my Father is the vinedresser." Jesus proceeds to reassure his disciples: "I am the vine, you are the branches. He who abides in me, and I in him, he it is that bears much fruit, for apart from me you can do nothing. If a man does not abide in me, he is cast forth as a branch and withers; and the branches are gathered, thrown into the fire and burned."

This simple parable, drawn from the vineyards of Palestine, tells the plain truth that the life of a disciple must bear fruit, but can do so only as it finds its nourishment in God's purpose. This is the ultimatum in the life and teachings of our Lord; the firm core of his challenge to his people and to his disciples. He was a man with a purpose—God's purpose for his life—and none could deflect him from it. Everyone had a try at it, sooner or later!

His family tried to get him to give up the public ministry and return to Nazareth. The firmness of his refusal borders on open rebuff to them. His fellow townspeople in Nazareth tried to belittle the high purpose

which was animating his life and thought, thereby to "take the wind
out of his sails," "bring him to his senses," rescue him from his foolish
notions and bring him back to their midst. He bluntly refused to listen
to them.

Time and again, his critics tried to confuse him about his purpose,
but he emerged from each encounter with purpose clear and firm.

His enemies threatened dire punishment if he did not give up his
mad conviction that in him God was actually ushering in a new age, a
new kingdom, a new being for man—but their threats fell on deaf ears.

In the days before the final trip to Jerusalem, he had left the relative
security of Galilee for the certain danger of Jerusalem despite his
disciples' entreaties to stay home. He set his face toward the Holy City
and they could either go along or stay behind, but he was going. Thomas
echoed the despair all seemed to feel: "Let us go with him that we may
die with him."

Jesus made it clear both by parable and in life that he was issuing an
ultimatum to mankind. History requires us to rephrase that and say:
"He was and is God's ultimatum to mankind." In him we see a purpose
—God's purpose—and we must choose whether or not to find our way
in that purpose.

Jesus expected his followers to lay their lives on the line. His firmness
on this point startles and sometimes offends the casual reader of the
Gospels. He warned them of the loneliness and costliness of discipleship
when he asked them to follow him. Later, when the going was tough,
none could say that he had either begged or coaxed them to come along.
In fact, he had warned them not to come unless they were willing to
leave all, to take up a cross daily, and to follow him. He *demanded*—
no softer word will do—he demanded that they come to him in a spirit
of complete commitment. They came, while we hesitate—and that, I
suspect, represents the big difference between discipleship then and
discipleship now.

II

The very word "commitment" grates on the ears of our generation.
We have been or think we have been schooled in the virtues of detachment, objectivity, and noninvolvement. When we consider the waves of
irrationality and hysteria that have gone and are continuing to go over

this generation, we are entitled to some doubts about the thoroughness of our devotion to these virtues. The fairer way to put it would run something like this if we should analyze our behavior honestly.

We believe in giving ourselves to social, political, and various humanitarian causes; we know that these cannot be furthered except people like us get in to them with a will and work with all their might. Knowing this, we do not hesitate to say that it is a shame to be objective and detached when they call for our loyalty and support. We know that we must give ourselves wholeheartedly to the mastery of the disciplines of our various professions if we are to achieve any kind of competency in them, and we think it a foolish sort of thing when a person will not do this.

I wish I could report that this same line of reasoning carried in matters of religion, but it does not. As a matter of fact, we think it is a sin to become deeply and personally involved in matters of religious faith. The late Dr. Henry Link, a consulting psychologist of wide repute in New York City, illustrates this point from his own experience in his book, *The Return to Religion*.

He tells of the relationship which he and his wife had to the church.

My wife in one of the great colleges for women, and I in one of the renowned colleges for men, received the Phi Beta Kappa keys. We both profited by our education to such an extent that we became virtual agnostics. If we believed in God at all, it was the most vague and attenuated kind of belief. Certainly it had nothing to do with the Church, the practices and preachings which had by this time become repugnant to us. We considered ourselves above such antics.[1]

The Links rested content in this detached state until their children came along. Then they found themselves unable to answer the children's questions about Sunday school and church, and began to debate whether or not they should send them along with neighboring children to church. They decided, as do a good many other parents, to be objective about this too—and let them go or not as they pleased. But the Links were exceptionally acute parents, and began to have their doubts about the wisdom of this course of action before long. Dr. Link finally decided to make some kind of study of what it means to a child's character to be related to the church. He devised a study that was given to two thousand children between the ages of ten and eighteen. The study has as its purpose the measurement of the personality traits of the children and the influences on these traits.

In his own words, Dr. Link says, "One of the most astounding results was the discovery that the most important habit contributing to an effective personality was going to Sunday school and having parents attend church." With that discovery, Dr. Link and his wife sent their children off to Sunday school and betook themselves to church even if, as he says quite candidly, "We did not like the idea at all, at first."

Every scientist, teacher, parent, and counselor knows that there is a time and place for detachment and objectivity in life. The wiser ones know, too, that there is a time and a place for devotion and commitment. The truly great leaders in any profession are much more than casual but proficient technicians; they are dedicated men and women—*dedicated to their task.* They may try to hide this sense of dedication behind a mask of depreciation, but it is there nonetheless. I cannot think of a single great relationship in life that can grow to its full stature of meaning without real commitment and dedication on the part of the participants. When people enter into marriage as a kind of trial run in intimate human relations, it is little more than a trial to both—and to everyone else, for that matter. But when they enter into it with a sense of dedication and commitment to the will of God which is seeking expression through their union, they break through the surface of the relationship and lose themselves in its divine depths, and find renewed life and love thereby.

The same thing is true of religion and the church. There is a time and a place for "shopping around" among various religions and churches. Tolerance and understanding require some experience that can come no other way. But there comes a time to stop this flitting about, to settle down and let the roots of one's life push their way deeply into the rich soil of a steady and continuing fellowship. Casual acquaintance can give you the forms of the church, but never the deep fellowship that is the true church. To adapt one of Edgar Guest's lines, "It takes a heap of living in a church to make it home." Any true revival of religion in our day will begin with this fact, and there is no real revival of religion apart from it.

III

Commitment, consecration, dedication—these words are inscribed over the door through which we enter into the Holy of Holies of religious experience. Turn anywhere we like in Christian history, whether in the New Testament or in any of the great epochs of our faith, and we are led to this door.

The New Testament scholar may revel in the richness, the beauty, and the simplicity of the language of the documents, he may enjoy the discipline of working with the manuscripts; he may take hold of them and work with them any way he will, but, finally, they will take hold of him and lead him to this door of commitment.

The careful historian of the Western world may devote himself to a detached, objective study of those tremendous periods when the Christian gospel, incarnate in men like Paul, Augustine, Luther, and Wesley, to name but a few, gave history a new turn, but, finally, with all his detachment and objectivity he, too, is led to this door. That is why Professor Hubert Butterfield, who occupies the distinguished chair of Modern History at Cambridge University in England, closes his book on *Christianity and History* in this interesting way:

I have nothing to say at the finish, except that if one wants a permanent rock in life and goes deep enough for it, it is difficult for historical events to shake it. . . . We can do worse than remember a principle which both gives us a firm rock and leaves us the maximum elasticity for our minds; the principle: *Hold to Christ, and for the rest be totally uncommitted.*[2]

But notice, if you will, that the very center of his life is complete commitment to the Christ—only then is it safe to be detached, objective, and uncommitted throughout the rest of life.

Nor can we who stand, or profess to stand, or would like to stand in the Christian tradition hope to escape the necessity of commitment. If we would understand the true nature of the gospel and the church, we are led to this door, even as were the disciples of old. If we would know the meaning of a Christian life, a Christian society, or of a Christian world, we come, finally and usually reluctantly, to this door of commitment. We must face the ultimatum which Christ always serves on those who would be his disciples: "I am the vine, you are the branches. . . . *apart from me you can do nothing.*"

As we might suppose, then, it is no casual experience to find ourselves at this door. No matter how many times we confront it—and we will be led to it repeatedly—we do so with the feeling that "this is it,"—one of those crucial moments of choice and decision which really give our life a new turn, if we have the will to enter, and, having entered, the strength to stay.

Jesus knew the comprehensiveness as well as the costliness of the commitment involved in his ultimatum. He had felt it in his own experience; he made it central in his teachings; his disciples might and did try to dodge it, but when they discovered what it meant, they entered, not counting the cost.

The parables that stress the urgency of commitment do not stand alone. When one of the learned men in religious circles asked Jesus to look over the many commandments which they had inherited from their fathers and single out the greatest one, Jesus drove to the heart of the matter with this imperishable insight: "You shall love the Lord your God with all your heart, and with all your soul, and with your mind. This is the great and first commandment. And a second is like it, you shall love your neighbor as yourself" (Matt. 22:37-39).

Each year when Lincoln's birthday rolls around, I read somewhere of his word that he would join any church that had this commandment of our Lord's for its creed. I need not tell you that I am a long-standing admirer of Lincoln and sympathize fully with his statement when it is set against the background of bickering over trivialities which characterized so much of formal religion in his time. I have so great a regard for him that I believe Lincoln actually meant it, and I believe he actually tried to do it. Which is to say that there is nothing trivial or casual about this summary of the meaning of religious faith, as both Jesus and Lincoln knew. That, I suppose, is why I find myself wondering whether people really understand it when they give the impression that it would be easier for them to belong to a church which had as a condition of entrance, Jesus' summary of the Law or one which asks you to believe in the Apostle's Creed or the Westminster Confession. If it were merely a matter of personal convenience, of picking the path of least resistance, of finding the easier way, I confess I would take the creeds and confessions—any or all of them—in preference to the narrow gate and the straight way indicated by our Lord.

It must have sent the chills up the spine of the family-conscious, home-loving Jews to hear Jesus say, "He who loves mother or father more than me is not worthy of me; and he who loves son or daughter more than me is not worthy of me; and he who does not take his cross and follow me is not worthy of me. He who finds his life will lose it, and he who loses his life for my sake will find it." Confronted by a spiritual and moral ultimatum like this, is it any wonder that his hearers deserted him in droves?

Who can miss the costliness of commitment when it lays the whole of life under the compulsion to love God with all one's heart, soul, mind, and strength? Who thinks that that will be easy? Can anything conceivably be harder? What a winnowing of ideas, plans, and purposes would take place in us if we sincerely tried to love God with all our mind! What a sorting over of impulse and desire would follow an honest effort to love God with all our heart! Try to love God with all our soul and the half-gods of parochial concerns and partisan ideals go, giving way to complete commitments to the one God who is the true Lord of all life.

Having brought all life under the judgment of the requirement to love God utterly, Jesus indicates the further requirement to love our neighbor as ourself.

I have sometimes heard this second commandment perverted into a curious plea for self-interest. There is no reason to think that Jesus ever merely accepted or tried to capitalize on our love of self. He knew us too well for that! He knew that we are easily pleased with ourselves, that we find it easy to grow very fond of ourselves—so fond, in fact, that we refuse to entertain the idea that we might be improved upon in any fundamental way. Actually, of course, Jesus was always trying to get men to improve upon themselves at all times and in every way. How could it be otherwise? The new relationship with God which he singles out as of paramount importance would result, he knew, in an utterly new being in man and an utterly new relationship among men.

He knew that the two could not be separated but had to be taken or left together.

We stand squarely upon the teachings of our Lord when we say that the Christian gospel requires commitment—and commitment means this: *A dedicated will, a dedicated mind, a dedicated society*—all dedicated to the proposition that men should seek first the kingdom of God, that they should seek to build a world where His will is done on earth even as it is in heaven.

IV

The very word "commitment" leaps with life. It means "to send together"; it is an act (1) of entrusting for safekeeping; (2) of actually doing something; (3) of engaging or pledging ourselves to do something.

Looking over the comprehensiveness and the costliness of this act of commitment, we find it easier to understand the note of anguish, yet of profound confidence, in the decisions that have loomed so large in the lives of our leaders in the Christian faith. Paul, I suspect, speaks for them all when he cries out, "But one thing I do, forgetting what lies behind and straining forward to what lies ahead, I press on toward the goal for the prize of the upward call of God in Christ Jesus" (Phil. 3:13-14).

There you have it: That keen consciousness of burning our bridges behind us, that cutting off of even precious ties that must be cut because they hinder the service of God, that forgetting of the things behind and a pressing forward in response to the call of God in Christ, this recentering of life around the one thing that stands out as supreme! Commitment means this or it means nothing worthwhile.

When we become Christian, we dedicate our minds to the service of the will of God as we see it in Jesus Christ. We cannot all become learned theologians like Thomas Aquinas or Paul Tillich, but we can be guided by the fixed star, "Ye shall know the truth and the truth shall make you free." We can rise to the high calling of believing that it is possible for us to have in us the mind that was in Christ Jesus. We can believe that we ought to try to "think God's thoughts after Him," as we seek to find our way in His will. The dedicated mind is conscious of the greater truth it seeks, of the ultimate truth it serves, of the eternal meanings it is trying to grasp. There is no room in it for conceit or pride, or even the prejudice that our little glimpse of truth presents the whole story. The dedicated mind is a humble mind, an aspiring mind, a searching mind, a mind that is conscious of its limitations even as it rejoices in the unlimited responsibilities given to it by life itself.

Commitment calls for a dedication of will, the ability to say, "Not my will but Thine be done." It is important but not enough to want to find God's truth; we must actually embark upon the search for it. It isn't enough to believe in, hope for, and pray for the kingdom of God; we must be so dedicated to it that we will work for it with every ounce of energy and every moment of time we have.

When in early colonial days, John Woolman, a lowly Quaker, set out to rid the Colonies of the curse of slavery, it must have seemed to his neighbors that it was an adventure in consummate conceit. By what right did this one man set himself up as judge of the morals and institutions of colonial society? By what kind of reasoning did he ever reach the conclusion that there was very much he could do about it, even if he disliked the institution of slavery? But, to me, the interesting thing about John Woolman was his confidence that when he had done his best, he had done all he was supposed to do—and that God would look after the rest. His will was so dedicated to God that it never occurred to him either that he could do the job alone or that the job would not be done because he could not do it. His faith in God more than made up for the deficiency he felt within himself and the unfinished tasks he knew would remain when he had finished.

Only as the members of a Christian church are dedicated to the Christ who calls them into being as churchmen can the church be Christian in intention or prayer or life. The church at the deepest level of her being is a fellowship of dedicated Christians who come together not alone to worship God but to stand in the white light of His judgment upon them, and to feel His directives to them in the light of the issues they face. We are not here to serve ourselves; we are here to serve God. Through the renewed dedication and commitment of ourselves to Christ and the kingdom he inaugurated, we seek to see ourselves as God sees us and to find our way in His will. There is need and room in this fellowship for all who are willing to submit to this experience of commitment. It is easy to think too much about the privilege of membership in the church and not enough about the responsibility of the privilege of membership in the church. And when we forget that responsibility, the judgment Bertrand Russell pronounced upon us rings with authenticity: "The Christian religion, as organized in its churches, has been and still is the principal enemy of moral progress in the world." That, clearly, was not the intention of our Lord. He was calling men into a way of life that would give them new goals to serve and new strength for serving. It is the witness of Christian experience that in our fellowship together in the service of His kingdom, we can find the deepest meaning of life.

A few miles outside Paris, Kentucky, in a grove of trees on a rural hilltop are a number of graves near the old Cane Ridge Meeting house where many a revival centered in the last century. On one of these stones is this inscription which I regard as an outstanding tribute to the meaning of churchmanship: "Here lies Nathaniel Rogers who was born in 1755. He was a member of the convention that formed the constitution of Kentucky in 1799. But what is of far more consequence, he was a member of the church of Christ in the bosom of which he died."

I should like to commend to all members of the church that phrase, "But what is of far more consequence, he was a member of the church . . ." This can be true of each one of us if we will accept the privilege and responsibility of commitment. There is an open door of Christian service before each person. No man can pass through it for another, nor can one force another to go through it against his will; each must choose to enter it himself. The church is the fellowship of those who have freely chosen to enter that door and to seek to find their way in His will.

14. Where Christianity Begins

MATTHEW 7:13-27

I

Beginnings, origins, fascinate many of us. I confess I am overcome *by them*—not only in religion but everywhere else. If I see a historical marker along a highway, I slow down and read it. When I see a plaque on a building I must know what it says. Should I learn that some movement, great or small, began there, we are through traveling for a while.

It is only human to want to see one's birthplace. Sometimes I feel sorry for our children who can only point to a towering hospital and say, "That is where I was born." Many of us can point to a farmhouse or house in a village as we say it. It is exciting to take one's children back to the family home and let them play where we played and see where we lived. There is something in life that seeks deep connections with the past as well as with the future.

The most exciting part of my first trip to the north woods in upper Minnesota many years ago came when the guide pointed to a small stream—one that could be easily spanned by a broad jump—and said, "This is where the Mississippi River begins." Having seen that mighty river in flood far down in the Southland, it seemed utterly incredible that I was looking at, and could jump across, the Mississippi. Yet even the mighty Mississippi must have a beginning somewhere.

Every visitor to New England wants to see—and should see—Plymouth Rock. It will be a sad day for everything America stands for if we forget what happened when the Pilgrims put their feet on that "stern and rockbound coast."

We have some very interesting beginnings in and around New York City. Recently I saw John Street Methodist Church for the first time and had no difficulty whatever recapturing, in imagination, that early day when the Methodist Church got its start in America. Every Methodist ought to go there not once but many times and see the various symbols of the beginnings of the movement: The chair of Captain Webb, the eloquent soldier-preacher who proclaimed the gospel along the waterfront; the clock sent by John Wesley; the Bible used by Philip Embury; the first pulpit used by the Methodist movement in this country—precious symbol of the genius of the church! I found it to be a wonderful restorer of vision clouded by detail and worry over the problems of Christ Church Methodist to go through John Street and recapture in imagination the day when Methodist work began in New York City.

All religions stress their beginnings and invite their followers to know and love them. Those of you who have been to the Holy Land know how moving an experience it is to be in Nazareth—where He was born and lived as a boy well into manhood; on the Mount— where He preached the Sermon; in Gethsemane—where He wrestled through to victory; on Calvary—where He died that we might live. Those of us who have not been there, if asked where on this earth we would like to go before we die, would say instantly, "The Holy Land." It is the land where Christianity began.

But, strictly speaking, Christianity began in a very special way—in the life and teachings of One who lived in that Holy Land. The first disciples were very practical men who had been plucked out of the very practical process of making a living one way and another and had been set on a strange and wonderful mission. This had happened because of One who said, "Follow me!" Follow him they did—but with questions and doubts forcing themselves to the surface all along the way.

Of course they were intrigued by Jesus' claim that he was inaugurating the age-old dream of the kingdom of God. How could they help being overwhelmed by the improbable possibility that he had called on them to share in this mighty accomplishment! But after their initial enthusiasm had worn off a bit, they found themselves facing some hard questions. What does this new kingdom demand of its citizens? What are we supposed to do? How will we be different from what we have been and from others because we are citizens of it?

Never one to demand blind faith, Jesus took them apart and taught them the meaning of discipleship. He did this through what we know as the Sermon on the Mount. They must have been thunderstruck at its austere demands—even as we are now.

The Sermon began with the Beatitudes as the goals or ideals of one who would perfectly fulfill the requirements of citizenship in the kingdom of God. Then the Teacher launched into a careful extension of the law from deed to motive. Murder is evil, as the law says, but so also are the hate and the anger which lead to it. Adultery is evil, but so also is the lustful spirit which causes it. Love of neighbor is good, but love of enemy is better. Jesus warns them of the perils that they face as they carry on. "Enter by the narrow gate: for the gate is wide and the way is easy that leads to destruction, and those who enter by it are many. For the gate is narrow and the way is hard that leads to life, and those who find it are few."

He gives them the test of good men: "You will know them by their fruits." And he urges them to be on guard against the permanent temptation of Christians—lip-service: "Not everyone who says to me, 'Lord, Lord,' shall enter the kingdom of heaven, but he who does the will of my Father who is in heaven."

Then he concludes with the parable of the two men, the two foundations, and the two houses, driving home the point that these teachings are to be taken seriously. They are not bypassed by lazy, timid disciples who want to relegate them to a never-never world rather than be guided by them in some serious fashion in this world. Few things could be clearer or more certain than that the writer of this Gospel as well as the early church expected Christians to begin here— with these teachings as guides to their daily life. Their witness was to be the life they lived in faithfulness to these teachings.

II

I find myself wondering whether people like us have the courage to let our Christianity begin in the Sermon on the Mount. Yet I confess that if it does not begin there, I do not know where else to say it takes its rise. We need, therefore, to raise in all seriousness the question of what it means to us today to take literally Jesus' insistence that true discipleship to him begins with these teachings. And what if we should?

One of the best answers to such doubts was given by a British scholar, John Hutton by name, many years ago. He faced up to them in what he called "The Proposal of Jesus." He said, "What our distracted world really needs is a complete submission of human motives to the will of God, a radical renovation of human society refashioning it upon the principle of faith in the righteousness of God. . . ." This is "the proposal of Jesus" as he came "to seek and to save that which was lost." Obviously, this proposal for the salvation of men and history is too probing to be reduced to, and then dismissed as, a platitude. It amounts to this: (1) to be saved, man must seek a new foundation for his life in the will of God; (2) to be saved, a society must seek a new foundation for its laws, conventions, and total life in the righteousness of God.

Such a proposal was laughed to scorn by the self-styled realists of Jesus' day—a fate which it has suffered almost uninterruptedly for nineteen centuries. And, more frequently than not, accredited leaders in the Christian churches have devised ways of tempering the high winds of his austere convictions to the shorn lambs of comfort-seeking Christians and outright pagans who want only to graze contentedly in the pastures of privilege. It has taken the combined and continuous efforts of a succession of prophetic spirits both inside and outside the church, to keep the gospel of salvation alive, and to proclaim it as "the Good News" to the whole world.

Of course Jesus was an idealist, but not one who was isolated from the realities of life. He was a prophetic idealist—peering intently into the depths of life, seeking to discern the movement and meaning of the will of God deep within events. He made his proposal to a world that was as tortured, distracted, and chaotic as ours today, and he made it in all seriousness, believing that it could and should be interpreted in terms of the great problem areas in human life and history. How else can we account for the urgency of this parable of the two foundations, the two builders, and the two houses which sums up the Sermon on the Mount? Nor do I know how to evade or blunt the urgency of the ethical imperatives which make that Sermon the most priceless deposit of religious insight known to man.

It does not ease my conscience one bit to have religious leaders tell me that in this world we are not supposed to try to be guided by the gospel of perfection which he preached. Of course, they hasten to add, we are to accept his teachings in principle as being true of the world if it were the world of God's intention, but we live in a far different world due to human sin. Therefore, we are counseled, we need not try to take Jesus' teachings as guides in actual practice.

This line of reasoning is wholly false. The simple truth is that Jesus intended that his teachings be taken seriously, and his hearers knew it too; therefore either they were repelled by what he said or they were led to follow him and try to do as he urged. Unless we accept his teachings as being relevant to the moral problems we face, they must be set aside as ethically irrelevant.

As a matter of fact, as we work our way into the meaning of Jesus' proposal for the world, we shall find it most relevant, bringing in fact a new sense of values and a new sense of direction, both of which we need if we are ever to get out of the cultural, moral, and political impasse in which civilization now finds itself.

He challenged men to take their stand on three basic principles: (1) God and His kingdom are the supreme facts in life and the world; (2) all men are His children; (3) life is a divine trust. These are not so much ideas to be weighed as paths to be followed. If we follow them to their end, we shall find ourselves in possession of a far different view of life and history than we now have, and, what is immeasurably more difficult, under the compulsion to be instruments of the redemptive will of God as He seeks to transform the world from what it is to what it ought to be.

When Jesus affirmed that God is the supreme fact in life and history, he was echoing the centuries-old faith of his forefathers. God is the Creator, Sustainer, and Redeemer of the world. No absentee Deity, His will for life is the deepest truth about it and should be sought with all diligence. His will is good; He can be trusted in all things both to sustain what is good and to rebuke and attempt to redeem what is evil. When man puts his trust in God and is able to keep it there, he becomes invulnerable to "the arrows of outrageous fortune," finding in God the strength he needs for living in adversity as well as in prosperity.

It follows, then, that all men are the children of God—rich and poor, good and evil, ill and well, joyful and sorrowful, white and colored—all are His children. This, I suppose, is one of our greatest needs—to know ourselves to be the sons of God. It is the only effective answer to the fear so well voiced by one of Dostoevski's agents in *The Brothers Karamazov*, "I am X in an indeterminate equation. I am a sort of phantom in life who has lost all beginning and end, and who has forgotten his own name."

There are many differentials in life, some more significant than others, to which we refer when we seek to "identify" ourselves. We may say we are white, or Methodist, or Catholic, or American; and such statements do indicate areas of relative importance. Yet will any deny that much if not most of the social tragedy of today grows out of the assumption that such differences which may set us apart in some identifiable way are more important than the things that actually unite us? If we accept these differences as being ultimately important, we will set out to transform the status quo until it reaches the point of our maximum advantage, and there we will try both to freeze it and to damn if not destroy anyone who tries to change it! Once accept these differentials as being more important than any other fact about us, and the stage is set for a continuation of man's inhumanity to man.

W. E. B. DuBois has described the true source of our trouble: "And herein lies the tragedy of the age: not that men are poor,—all men know something of poverty; not that men are wicked,—who is good? not that men are ignorant,—what is Truth? Nay, but that men know so little of men."[1]

And it is just this knowledge that Jesus' proposal calls to our attention. For deeper than the things which separate us is this fact which binds us in an unbreakable unity: We are the children of God. Any purpose, plan, policy, convention, law, person, or institution which does not base itself upon this foundation is candidate for conversion by the gospel of salvation.

When we accept ourself and others as children of God, our life acquires a new source of meaning, worth, and purpose. And with it comes a new sense of tolerance, humility, and understanding—for no one knows God perfectly and no one has lost Him completely. God is too great, too good, for the wisest and best of us to be able to say of Him, "We know Him as He is." He is too loving, too compassionate to forsake even the worst of us, the difference between sinner and saint being always a matter of degree and never one of kind. God's rain and sunshine fall upon the just and the unjust alike. Where in this is there room for self-righteousness and pride—those twin distorters of a proper estimate of another? Where is there room for the depersonalization of man which has been so marked a characteristic of the economic and international policies of modern history?

Pascal caught the spirit of our Lord's proposals truly when he wrote in *Pensées,* "Let man know his value. Let him love himself, for there is in him a nature capable of good; but let him not, for this reason, love the vileness that is in him." When the Christian faith tells us that we are the children of God, it is trying to teach us the true foundation for valuing ourselves and others. It saves us from the cry of desperation which produces confessions like this: "For all of us, from the most intelligent to the least intelligent, are weary of the materialist pummeling we have received during the last seventy or eighty years. . . ." And unless we can be delivered from this sort of despair and lifted to a new plateau of understanding about ourselves, we are lost indeed.

Implicit in the conviction that God is the supreme fact in life and history and that all men are the children of God is the claim that life is a divine trust. Life, everyday living, is a dealing with God. Life is our truest word to and from God. For Jesus, words, as words, did not carry much weight. The deed—that is the real revelation of a man's faith. "By their fruits ye shall know them," is Jesus' timeworn admonition. Our possessions and human relationships are sacred in the exact sense that they involve the divine intention as truly as our own. Property, food, clothing, security—all these are important providing they do not become ends in themselves but actually bring men closer to the kingdom of God. But the kingdom of God must come first in a man's thought and life if he would correctly appraise himself and his work. When a man sees in bigger granaries ease of soul, he has lost his soul. When a man's anxiety about tomorrow takes possession of him, he loses today as well as tomorrow. When a man worries so much about food and clothing that he forgets the purpose of life itself, he has not kept first things first.

Thus Jesus went through the great fears and worries of men pointing out the plain fact that faith in the fact and the reality of the will of God is the real and the only answer. Long before Dostoevski in *The Brothers Karamazov,* he saw this truth: "For the secret of man's being is not only to live but to have something to live for. Without a stable conception of the object of life, man would not consent to go on living, and would rather destroy himself than remain on earth, though he had bread in abundance." There are, of course, two alternatives other than those suggested by the Russian novelist. One is to be found in the popular conviction that we make up our own rules and are at liberty therefore to live for any end we choose, be it mountain or molehill. The other is expressed in the beautifully phrased confession of a literary critic: "People like myself have got to take a direction finally; we can't go on forever being bright or smart or naughty young things."

Such alternatives are futile because they are false. The fact of God, the reality of His claim on us gives the lie to them. Yet we can be saved from them only as we come to terms with God and His will for us— of this Jesus was certain. Beginning with that little company assembled on the mountaintop to hear him outline the meaning of the kingdom, millions of Christians have found good reason to share his faith.

How well we know that the human situation rapidly becomes intolerable unless life is treated as a divine trust. Treat other persons or races or nations as means to our end, as instruments in purposes that serve our own welfare, and to the extent that we are successful, we make revolutions inevitable. Yet the illusions nourished by power, wealth, and position continue to darken our awareness of this fact. The ability to enforce our will on others through military power is such an impressive fact today that we are turning to it as a kind of guarantor of security. Might, more might; power, more power; bombs, more bombs—that is the dominant cry and desperate hope of altogether too many of us. We seem to agree with a certain news commentator who in advocating a get-tough line in world affairs exclaimed, "We are the masters of our fate. History is what men make it. If we do not choose to get out and make it what we want, at whatever cost, it is going to be made for us by other men who are willing to work at it."

It cannot be said too firmly: Such counsel is more than futile; it is fatal. To say that history is what we make it is to utter a most dangerous half truth, the full version of which is this: History is what God permits us to make it. History is the scene of our dealings with God and His with us. It is true that we are free to try to build any kind of social order we choose or any kind of world we want, but the validity of our plan and the permanence of our building are determined by a power entirely beyond our control. James Anthony Froude, after a lifetime spent in the study of history, bears this impressive witness: "One lesson and one only history may be said to repeat with distinctness; that the world is built somehow on moral foundations; that in the long run it is well with the good; in the long run it is ill with the wicked."

III

Not for a moment did our Lord seek to hide from his disciples the costliness of such convictions. The transformation of life and history plainly implicit in them calls for more than a verbal proclamation of them; they had to "come alive," to become incarnate in the lives of men and in history before they could become the way of salvation. He made it clear that one could know the vocabulary of religion, could say, "Lord, Lord," yet not know or be known by its transforming power. Looking back upon the faith of Jesus as he went among his fellows and on the fate they meted out to him, Paul counseled his hearers to remember, "Ye are bought with a price." The cross became the symbol not alone of the fate of Jesus but of the price which any man who follows him must be prepared to pay. Whether the gospel of salvation spreads slowly or rapidly, every inch of advance is "bought with a price"—that is the unqualified testimony of nineteen hundred years of Christian history.

Where does Christianity begin? In loyalty to Jesus Christ as the revelation of God's will for man's life; in belief in his teachings; in commitment to him as our Lord and our Leader. And in fellowship with those who followed him to the mountaintop to hear the Sermon, and then down into the valley to meet the challenge of daily human needs. As we do this, we will be like the wise man who built his house on a rock.

15. Shall We Be Patient with Evil?

MATTHEW 13:24-30

I

How shall we deal with evil? This question has perplexed men from the beginning of time. It aggravated Plato and it writes today's headlines. It has pressed in upon the Christian conscience with special intensity from the day Jesus addressed this parable to his disciples:

The kingdom of heaven may be compared to a man who sowed good seed in his field; but while men were sleeping, his enemy came and sowed weeds among the wheat, and went away. So when the plants came up and bore grain, then the weeds appeared also. And the servants of the house-holder came and said to him, Sir, did you not sow good seed in your field? How then has it weeds? He said to them, An enemy has done this. The servants said to him, Then do you want us to go and gather them? But he said, No; lest in gathering the weeds you root up the wheat along with them. Let both grow together until the harvest; and at harvest time I will tell the reapers, gather the weeds first and bind them in bundles to be burned, but gather the wheat into my barn (Matt. 13:24-30).

This story, like all parables of our Lord, comes straight from the life of his own day and people. A man sowed his field with good grain and then went to sleep. As he slept, an enemy sprinkled the field with a seed which produced a weed that, in its early stages, so resembled wheat that the two could hardly be told apart. As they grew, discerning servants suspected that something was wrong and brought word of it to the farmer. After a quick look, he agreed with them that an enemy had tried to ruin the crop. What should he do? Go over the field and pull up the weeds? No—that would ruin the good grain. There was only one thing to do: "Let both grow together until the harvest"—when the separation can and will be made.

This incident could not have occurred in the wheat-growing sections of America where farms stretch over hundreds of acres and the sowing of a crop requires time and complicated machinery, but it could happen in a small country like Palestine where farm land was scarce and individual tracts small, with sowing and reaping done by hand.

There was a well-known weed, a poisonous, bearded darnel that looked so much like wheat that the Rabbis called it "a perverted kind of wheat." Obviously Jesus' parable would appeal to an audience composed of people who knew how easy it was for an enemy to destroy a crop by a night foray into their small fields. And his advice to "let both grow together until the harvest" must have seemed the summit of good sense to them. In a hand-labor farm economy where every stalk of grain was handled in the harvest, the sorting could be done, and the good wheat could be saved.

Now we come to a more difficult point: Why did Jesus use this parable? What was he trying to say with it? Here scholars are in serious disagreement.

Some say he was debating the question of what to do with Judas Iscariot who was already showing signs of defection. Should he send him packing? If he did, what would be the effect of this dismissal on the ones who remained? "Perhaps we ought to let him stay until we're sure he is no longer one of us," he reasoned. "Then it will be time enough to tell him to leave the group."

The early church treasured the parable and used it steadily as they tried to deal with the conflict between evildoers in their fellowship and the purists who wanted to throw them out. This controversy rumbles through Paul's letters like thunder in distant hills. Paul makes it plain that he is on the side of patience. He would subscribe to our Lord's admonition, "Let both grow together until the harvest." Evildoers are to be warned, prayed over, given every chance to mend their ways, and, only as a last resort, asked to leave the fellowship.

Three hundred years later Augustine, when confronting a similar situation, fell back on the parable for guidance. A group of intense Christians, indignant with what they regarded as the toleration of heresy in the church, raised the cry, "Purify the church," and advocated an all-out persecution of anyone suspected of dangerous thoughts and practices. Augustine took issue with them, not because he was a friend of heresy, but because he did not want the church destroyed by civil strife and the Christian fellowship broken by increasing hatred. As I read his handling of the matter, I get the impression that while he agreed in principle with those who wanted to pull up the weeds, he was not sure he knew the difference between the weeds and the wheat in any given case. So he cried, "Let both grow together until the harvest."

The sheer power of this parable will come through to anyone who gives it careful examination. In a half dozen sentences it suggests almost as many fundamental truths about the proper relationship between God, man, and evil:

1. Good and evil are real facts to be encountered and dealt with.

2. Good and evil are, finally, as different as weeds and wheat—there is no ultimate confusion about which is which.

3. There is need for the wisdom and the patience of God in dealing with evil.

4. Man alone is neither capable of, nor able to, root out evil; only God can do that.

5. Hardest of all, man must accept the inevitable interval involved in the growth of good and evil to that point where they can be identified and dealt with.

There is a time for planting and a time for harvesting, and stretching between the two is the inevitable interval—a time for patient waiting during which the plant grows, and the determination of its true nature is made. It is the counsel of our Lord that we should "let both grow together to the harvest," and then the separation can be made.

Which, as I understand it, is a way of saying that there is no place for snap judgments in God's dealing with the world, even with the evil in the world. Why do we who seek to think His thoughts after Him have so much trouble with this? Have we not said and tried to believe that He sends His rain upon the just and the unjust alike? Did He not send His Son to call the sinners as well as the righteous to repentance? Are we not all grateful to God that there is no quick writing-off of any one of us as being "hopeless" or "lost" or "worthless"? The point of the parable is clear: God insists on being fair to evil as well as to good until the full nature of both can be determined. This is not a way of coddling evil; it is the only known way of protecting the good.

II

Stand on this insight of our Lord which towers above the landscape of the way we usually do things, and we get a different perspective on people and events.

Take the Civil War, for example. Like you, I have been doing a fair amount of reading in that period of our history and I am appalled not only at the accepted attitudes on both sides then, but also by the changes that have come about in less than a hundred years. Everything was crystal-clear then—on both sides—if we may judge by what they were saying. It was a time of black-and-white judgments. You were for or against—"perhaps" was not admitted. It was a time of sharp, clear, harsh, snap judgments on "people, places, and things."

But something has happened during the interval of nearly a century since that dark day. Last summer, while in Harrisburg, Pennsylvania, I went to the old capitol building, now a museum, to study again the huge painting of Pickett's Charge at Gettysburg. In front of me, a mother and two small sons were seated, looking at the picture. The older boy asked, "Which are the goodies and the baddies in that picture?" His mother replied softly, "It's hard to tell." "Why are they trying to kill each other?" the boy persisted. The mother answered slowly, telling about slavery and other troubles. "Did they have to fight?" the lad asked. And I treasure her reply: "They thought so." There was in that reply the gentleness distilled in the interval of a hundred years. Gone the sharpness, the harshness of snap judgments —now, an awareness not only of the evil of slavery but also of the equally great evil of what can only be called the will to misunderstand, to misrepresent, and to misjudge people who disagree with us. If evidence were needed for the adage, "Two wrongs do not make a right," I would submit this tragic chapter from the experience of our country.

Many other such chapters might be submitted from other areas of human experience. In fact, wherever people impatiently brush past the inevitable interval of growth and break forth with snap judgments, another chapter is in the making.

Why do we act this way? The answer is not easy. Sometimes because we are afraid of the changes proposed by those who differ, and fear is always a risky guide. Sometimes because we do not take the time to be sure before we make up our minds. Socrates once observed, "He who takes only a few things into account finds it easy to pronounce judgment."

To talk this way is not a poorly disguised plea to be soft with evil; it is an open plea that we seek to be sure that evil is actually evil before we move in on it, lest we destroy the good as well. And we have reason enough to be cautious on this matter. The policy of "wait and see" may not please the young Julians of the world who cry, "Let me go forth and purge the world," and launch a reign of naked persecution of all who differ, but it will commend itself to anyone who has studied the way in which the "dangerous radicals" of one generation become the "founding fathers" by the next.

Recall how the young radicals who clustered around William and Mary College in Williamsburg, Virginia, in colonial days became the Founding Fathers of the Declaration of Independence and formed the key ideas of the Constitution of the United States. They were, in truth, the grand architects of many of our basic institutions. Rebels with a price on their heads for awhile, yet respected and revered later on—thus the wheel of history turns under the impulse of God's patience and love.

III

The implications of all this will not be lost on persons in positions of responsibility in our colleges and universities as well as in our churches and other public institutions.

Every wise college president with an eye to the genius of his school knows that he must always be on the lookout and guard jealously the right of his teachers to grow toward the full maturity of their thought. He must fight off misguided individuals who want to rush into a faculty and uproot the dangerous ideas and radical thinkers who occasionally are found there. These well-intentioned individuals are like the servants who wanted to rush into the field and tear up the weeds even though they were not quite sure which were weeds and which wheat; even though they knew that to root up one would probably kill the other. Even as it was the part of wisdom then to "let both grow together to the harvest" it is the part of wisdom for a great center of learning to prize criticism and differences of opinion as essential to its very soul. And we ought to honor institutions that do this in the face of even the biting criticism of Congressional committees that, of late, have been all too much in evidence in their determination to dominate the educational institutions of America.

Every lover of civil liberties will want to take to heart this insight of our Lord into God's way of working with the world. We have seen it demonstrated a dozen times over the last half century that men can lose freedom either by overthrow from without or by betrayal of the spirit of freedom within their own country. We have it in the words of J. Edgar Hoover, of Dwight D. Eisenhower, and of the Attorney General Robert Kennedy that the fear of Communism now poses a greater threat to American civil liberties than Communism itself. No one can question the simple fact that Communism would put an end to what we know as a free society. It has done so many times and will do so again if and where it can. But many who know this will not face the equally plain fact that the fear of Communism has betrayed and will continue to betray us into snap judgments which equate serious criticism of our way of life with treason. We have slipped a long way from Justice Oliver Wendell Holmes' "Golden Rule for freedom of thought": "not free thought for those who agree with us but freedom for the thought we hate."

Writing in 1952, Justice Learned Hand observed,

We are in the distressing position of all who find their axioms doubted: . . . And we have responded as men generally do respond to such provocation: for the most part we seem to be able to think of nothing better than repression; we seek to extirpate the heresies and wreak vengeance on the heretics. . . . the doctrines that so frighten us constitute a faith, which we must match with a faith, held with equal ardor and conviction. So we are repeatedly assured, and rightly assured; but what we much less often observe is that, in making use of our faith as a defence, we may be in danger of destroying its foundations and abandoning its postulates.[1]

IV

Patience—great patience—patience akin to that of God is essential to the building of anything worthwhile—especially the greatest thing of all, the kingdom of God. Even as Rome was not built in a day, the kingdom of love cannot be hurried and shoved into being by fretful, self-righteous, hasty "men in a hurry." How clearly Jesus saw that!

We need his kind of patience if we are to be workers together with

God in the building of that kingdom. His was a positive, radiant grace flowing from the awareness of the greatness and the goodness of God. Believing that God was working a mighty work of redemption through him, he gave himself to the realization and fulfillment of that work. Lying deep beneath all that happened to him was this confidence that "I work and my Father worketh in me."

That must have been the source of his patience in working with the disciples. He spent untold hours with them, answering their questions, training them to think, to feel, and to pray for the kingdom. When they deserted him at the end, he must have wondered whether his faith had been misplaced. But he had been right: Like a mighty magnet, it drew them together and to him and to the work of the kingdom again.

The disciples, like us, wanted to get things done in a hurry. Some thought the kingdom would come right away. When it did not, many concluded that their faith had been misplaced and they left the fellowship. Others concluded that time was on God's side and that He would use whatever amount of it He needed in the building of the kingdom. Thereupon they began to do two things that belong together in Christian ethics: "wait and see" and "work and pray." This is not quietism, a folding of the hands in moral irresponsibility; rather it is a clear recognition that all great undertakings take time—and the work of the kingdom may take eternity—only God knows.

Patience, so conceived, does not mean being soft with evil or sentimental about evildoers. Rather patience requires firmness—the firmness of conviction, purpose, and loyalty. But a firmness tempered by gentleness—a gentleness born of an awareness of the need for time in which the evil can grow to the point where it may be distinguished and overcome.

Cancer is a very great evil, and the conquest of it will surely come, but the ones who will win that victory—rather who are winning it— are not impatient, fretful men, but men of infinite patience in laboratory and hospital. Money is needed, of course, but mountains of money of itself will not win the victory. Nor will pep talks and torchlight parades help much. Firmness, patience, persistence, understanding— these are essential ingredients of the victory, and they take time.

As with cancer of the physical tissue so it is with evil ideologies that challenge everything we stand for: Firmness, patience, and understanding operating steadily in our thought and life—these will win or the victory will never be won. This is no time to lose patience with Russia, or Red China, or Fidel Castro in our effort to hurry along a complete victory over them. As surely as we do that, we shall find ourselves tempted to risk or actually to take dangerous steps that will seriously imperil the precarious balance of peace and heighten the risk of irrevocable disaster.

Patience is not softness due to lack of conviction; patience is firmness born of conviction and sustained by a purpose guided by a gentleness which knows that time and persistence are essentials of all enduring victories.

The question, "Shall we be patient with evil?" admits of only one answer when held in the light of the Christian ethic: "Yes—as patient as God is with sinners like us and the evil in our lives."

What a different kind of home, church, community, and world we would have if the human point of this parable could get through to our calloused consciences and hard hearts. No more snap judgments! No more hurrying from headline to headline in frantic haste! No more execution of character by hearsay and gossip when someone disagrees with us even in fundamental matters! None of these, but a willingness to let both grow together to the harvest and the infinite patience to let the truth be proved in the event itself.

V

Truly we need something of the patience of God if we are to live with each other. As well we know, it is hard to be honest with other persons—especially those who disagree with us. Yet we know from the snap judgments which people pass on us and which we have passed on other people how utterly unfair they usually are. Here, as elsewhere, Jesus shows us the way.

He heard the word "sinner" applied freely to persons round about him. And it was more than a word then. It had real bite to it. It indicated someone you could not associate with or exchange greetings with, even though you knew him by name. You would deny every form of deep fellowship with him. To call a person a sinner was to make him an outcast—and you were supposed to separate yourself voluntarily from all relationships with him. It is a striking thing that our Lord paid little or no attention to the distinctions that were sup-

posed to separate sinners and saints. He knew that there was much
more to a person than any sin he might have committed. He was a
child of God, a person who needed God, a creature in search of his
Creator, a child in need of his Father and—lest we forget—a human
being in need of a friend. Jesus took the time, in loving patience, to
know the sinner in this deeper dimension of his being—his spirit and
soul—and he loved him all the more because of his need. That is why
Jesus lived in a different ethical world from that of the custodians of
accepted religious ethics in his day.

How can we escape the conviction that this is the clue to Christian
ethics in personal relationships and world policies alike? We are not
called upon to build a kingdom of God with rack and screw, nor even
with fear and bombs. We are not called upon to scare people into the
kingdom by parading the terrors of Hell before them—as lingering
revivalists are wont to do. Rather we are called upon to believe and to
incarnate as best we can a simple yet divinely inspired truth: "God
so loved the world that he gave his only Son, that whoever believes
in him should not perish but have eternal life" (John 3:16).

Whatever else this may mean, it cannot be fashioned into a club
for pounding people into the kingdom of God. Nor is it a man-made
mold into which we pour human beings in order to shape and form
them to our own desires. It is the worst text imaginable for the heresy
hunters and the grand inquisitors who seem to be springing up like
poisonous mushrooms in all walks of life these days.

Rather it puts its finger squarely on the great event which we
celebrate in the gospel and in the Christian church, namely, the love
of God for all men in Christ. And it gives us a message to believe, to
live, and to share with others—all others.

Someone once warned the church, "We are called to build temples,
not to whittle sticks." An irritable, impatient, short-tempered man can
whittle sticks, but he is of little use in the building of a temple like
the kingdom of God. That calls for a plan—God's plan; it calls for
patience—God's patience; it calls for the strength of tenderness and
understanding which refuses to shut any man out, to give anyone up
for lost. And it calls for one thing more—the willingness to let God
be the final Judge of men, and not to invade the sanctuary of that awful
responsibility with our ignorance, sinfulness, and blindness. We are
called upon to overcome evil with good—and that takes both the

patience and the love of God actually at work in and through persons like ourselves.

If someone should ask how much of this we may honestly expect to be able to do, I can only reply by means of the story of a Red Cross worker among refugees who handed a little boy a glass of milk. He looked at it hungrily, silent for a moment, then asked softly, "How deep shall I drink, Ma'am?" "Drink as deep as you can, Son, as deep as you can," she said. So it is and must ever be with the patience and the love of God which come to us in Jesus Christ: "How much of that am I supposed to have?" we ask. And the reply is, "As much as you can."

16. Humility Is an Essential Christian Virtue

LUKE 14:7-11

I

The ancient prescription of humility is bitter medicine for mortals like us: so bitter, in fact, that we seldom take it. We much prefer the taste of pride. And it must be one or the other—pride or humility —between them we must choose as we shape our code of values for living. They know each other to be mortal foes; they cannot inhabit the same person or live in the same world. But this is no new conflict for Christians to feel and to face.

The early Christian preachers of humility were ridiculed by the proud Greeks and Romans as those who appealed to the "dregs of the populace," to slaves, criminals, children, and to simple-minded women. Their scoffers argued that no rational man could regard humility as a virtue. The very words "humble" and "humility" were tossed into a general category of highly unsavory words like "meek," "lowly," "despised," "downtrodden."

Yet the Christian preachers met this storm of criticism with the firm insistence that humility is a Christian virtue and essential to the Christian life. They had good biblical backing for their position. There was Micah's famous admonition: "What does the Lord require of you but to do justice, and to love kindness, and to walk humbly with your God?" (Mic. 6:8.) There was the beatitude: "Blessed are the meek, for they shall inherit the earth" (Matt. 5:5).

They must have found great strength in the parable of our Lord which centers in a wedding feast. As in so many of the parables, Jesus was trying to drive home a point to his major critics, the scribes and the Pharisees.

This is how Luke reconstructs the story of what must have been a most interesting dinner party:

Now he told a parable to those who were invited, when he marked how they chose the places of honor, saying to them, When you are invited by any one to a marriage feast, do not sit down in a place of honor, lest a more eminent man than you be invited by him; and he who invited you both will come and say to you, Give place to this man, and then you will begin with shame to take the lowest place. But when you are invited, go and sit in the lowest place, so that when your host comes he may say to you, Friend, go up higher; then you will be honored in the presence of all who sit at table with you. For every one who exalts himself will be humbled, and he who humbles himself will be exalted (Luke 14:7-11).

Obviously our Lord's keen eye missed no detail in this memorable feast. He saw how unconsciously the Pharisees went to the seats near the host, simply assuming that places of honor were for them. If not for them, then for whom? Therefore, without a trace of false modesty, they took their places and let the rest of the company fend for themselves. There is no suggestion that anyone challenged what they did. But the profound spiritual meaning of their behavior was not lost on the young Galilean whose mind was dark with anxiety over the unfitness of such religious leaders to participate in the life and work of the kingdom of God which he was proclaiming. Reluctant to give them up, he tested their spirit with a series of parables, one of which centers in a wedding feast.

Ostensibly, he was making a point in proper etiquette on such an occasion: Wait for the host to arrange guests according to his own desires and judgment. If you assume your own importance and make for a place of honor, you may very well be embarrassed by being asked to give way to one who, in the judgment of the host, is more deserving of it. It is wiser, he said, to take the least distinguished seats. Then, if you are surprised, it will be a pleasant one.

Actually, he was not discussing etiquette at all. He did not care two figs about who sat where upon such occasions. But he was deeply concerned over the way pride had corrupted the faith of the religious leaders of his people. His was not simply a counsel of prudence on how to avoid humiliation in a social gathering. It was a searching insight into the spiritual nature of someone who yearns for the head table, the seat of honor, and who believes he has earned the right to sit there.

The Pharisees could not have missed his point. He was telling them in the plainest way possible that there is no place for their pride in status, their assumption of honor, in the kingdom of God. For in that kingdom, God will seat people as He thinks they deserve, and a humble man will fare better than a proud one. Jesus gives them this prescription for humility: "For everyone who exalts himself will be humbled, and he who humbles himself will be exalted."

Understandably, the early church relied heavily on this broad biblical foundation in its insistence that humility is a necessary virtue.

Augustine, easily the greatest of the Latin Fathers, said, "Should you ask me, What is the first thing in religion? I should reply, 'The first, second and third thing therein—nay, all—is humility.'" I do not know of a single religious classic written during the two thousand years of Christian history that does not place a similar high valuation on humility. Thomas À Kempis in his *Imitation of Christ* speaks for all: "God walks with the humble; He reveals himself to the lowly; He gives understanding to the little ones; He discloses His meanings to pure minds; but hides His graces from the curious and the proud."

II

We might hope that so consistently strong an emphasis over nearly two thousand years would have made a distinct impression by now. Some Christian valuations have registered in the conscience of man, but not humility. We have always resisted it—and successfully. And we continue to kick against its pricks, and exalt pride as a virtue.

Obviously we are confronted with something far more serious than a theoretical problem. It is as practical a one as we will face—if we have the courage to face it. "Pride," the word, is no vice; "humility," the word, is no virtue. But when pride and humility are incarnate in human lives, they become an evil person or a good person; someone we can live with in understanding, or someone we are afraid to be around lest he take advantage of us and use us to serve his own ends.

It is hard to say when the elevation of pride from vice to virtue took place, but it seems to have infected all to some degree. While pride is not our only vice, it is easily one of the most dangerous, and, to make matters worse, it garbs itself as a virtue. Pride in country, pride in culture, pride in background, pride in church, pride in human achievements—are we not all moved by these powerful forces? I cannot say such appeals are wholly evil, but I am making the point— rather history is making the point—that the good in them is always threatened and usually overcome by the evil; that they inevitably produce a sense of superiority and tend toward the creation of conflict.

I do not know why it is so, but we seem to be unable simply to be proud of our own way of life; we feel we must exalt it above other ways of life. We cannot simply be proud of our church; we feel we must exalt it above other churches. We cannot simply be proud of the values we cherish and seek in our culture; we must, somehow or other, exalt them above the values prized in other cultures.

It is a depressing experience to come home from a visit to another country where you have sensed the richness of their culture and religious heritage and meet questions like these: "But isn't our way of life better? Isn't our religion truer?" Though I am inclined to say "Yes," I am suspicious both of my reasons and of the speed with which I want to answer. It is easy for pride to blind us—but that's pride for you. *It always blinds,* and it is blinding us in so many obvious ways today!

Humility is essential to honesty—the kind of sincere searching honesty that alone can keep pride from blinding us to our vices as well as to the virtues of others. We have seen the need for this written large in the grudging way the United States and Russia have acknowledged each other's achievements in the field of space research and exploration. How differently we would feel about it all if we had invited the astronauts and cosmonauts to visit each other's land, and gave each the same hero's welcome. But no—we must think of each other as deadly enemies: We must look at every achievement of the other with eyes heavy with hate and suspicion. Only humility can free us from such blindness and enable us to rejoice in the great gifts and achievements of one another.

III

We live in a stricken world; so stricken that finally, we may be willing to learn things which up to now we have been unwilling to look at for more than a moment.

We are so chastened that should someone argue that our culture is simply barbarism in the clothing of civilization, we may enter a demurrer but not a denial. Our science, instead of being a monumental achievement to the creative genius of men, has made us the deadliest animal ever to live on the face of this earth. Our philosophy, instead of bringing life under careful, constructive criticism, has usually tended to embrace and explain away our brutality, sugar-coat our inhumanity, and wherever possible, take the glory and the glow out of our religious faith. Our religion has all too frequently been called upon to pour holy water on our brutality even to the point of bringing the blessings of a God of peace and love upon the conflicts and the hatreds of men.

So far as I can see, both the earlier optimism and the prevailing pessimism about man ought to be rejected. I suggest that the quickest way to accomplish this is to re-examine the meaning of Jesus' prescription for humility: "Everyone who exalts himself will be humbled and he who humbles himself will be exalted."

IV

If we put the Christian insistence on humility in a single sentence, it would read something like this: *Humility is the way we feel when we see ourselves as a part of God's world.* Christianity has never argued that we ought to be humble; it has simply insisted on placing us in a perspective that would make us humble. Humility is the only honest reaction of a person who sees himself as a part of God's world and feels God's claim on him.

In my study, I have a book of maps in which the City of New York appears in various perspectives. One map is devoted solely to the City of New York. As I study it, I might be excused for thinking New York quite a place. A second map is of the United States, and I find a little more difficulty in locating New York on it. But I can find it! Standing above these maps is a globe, and I may as well admit that it's difficult to locate New York on it. And now the cosmonauts and the astronauts will soon be presenting us with a map of interplanetary if not interstellar spaces—and I am sure no one will think me disloyal to New York when I say I doubt very much whether we will be able to find New York on that one. Each time the area presented on the map is enlarged, the relative importance of the size of New York City is diminished.

In similar fashion humility urges us to see ourselves in the perspective of God's total universe. Only then can we get a proper perspective upon ourselves; see the true meaning of our own life as it really is in the pure light of the holiness of God. Nor is there any way in which we can measure the worth of the civilization which we are trying to build except we measure it against His intention in the kingdom of God.

Humility is the way we feel when we see ourselves in the total perspective of God's will. That is why it is necessary to our noblest enterprises. It is the breath of life to science and any form of careful investigation. It provides the only atmosphere with high enough oxygen content to permit an education to breathe. It is not uncommon to find an education embalmed in the conceit of its owner. Educators have always known that conceit will put an end to one's education quicker than anything else.

William James, one of our greatest thinkers, was humble enough to be a learner all his life. He would listen to anyone who could talk intelligently. Upon one occasion, he failed to show up at a tea given in his honor. Anxious friends found him deeply engrossed in conversation with a man in charge of the work crew widening one of the streets of Boston. James would have understood the motto that a French scientist, Charcot by name, put over the door of his laboratory: "My work is bigger than myself."

Humility is essential to appreciation as well as to investigation. The artist comes to mind as we think of one who is skilled in appreciation. As nearly as I can determine from watching artists work through many different media, there are certain things they do before they ever touch the materials with which they are to work. *First,* they observe with care. *Second,* they study with patience. *Third,* they achieve a certain perspective or understanding of their subject. *Finally,* they tell us as best they can what they see or feel to be important about it. Though artists as men may be proud as peacocks, artists at work are humility incarnate.

We who are not creative artists but desire an intelligent appreciation of their works must be humble, too, if we are going to discover what it is they are trying to say. We, too, must observe, study, understand, and share. And as we do, we will appreciate the gentle words spoken by a guide in the Art Institute of Chicago to some high school students who asked what a certain painting "meant": "Keep looking at it over the years. Its meaning will grow on you," he said.

Humility, the virtue of seeing ourselves in the largest possible perspective, is essential to co-operation throughout life. The big problems that confront us today are essentially those of co-operation: *the recognition of the right and privilege of others to share responsibility and reward in this business of living together.*

Coercion is a form of co-operation, I suppose, since it is a way of living together—but it is easily the lowest type of co-operation. It consists largely in shoving people around. Coercion is essential to the maintenance of society on a rudimentary level—this, we know. We need police and courts and prisons and all the paraphernalia of law and order to have a society, but a social order which proceeds solely by coercive means is the lowest form of society. In fact, the whole thrust of civilization away from barbarism must be read as an attempt to move from a coercive to a co-operative society. And although Christians have been laughed to scorn when they talk about the kingdom of God as though it were something more than an idle dream, we continue to struggle for a society in which the will of God binds all men into a human family.

Few people question the need for co-operation in a stable marriage and home. Some time ago I had a conference with a couple who were to be married. The man was from the deep South and a conservative religious background. The father wrote his son asking him to be sure the word "obey" was either in or would be put in the pledge which the bride would make. I could only say, "We have not used that in our pledge for over thirty years."

"Co-operate" is a better word than "obey" any and every day of the week in a Christian home; yet we cannot have co-operation between human beings without humility in the hearts of all. When anyone sets himself up as a final judge and arbiter of everything that happens in an intimate human relationship, the relationship is impoverished thereby. Humility, the willingness to see oneself as an essential part, but as only one of the essential parts, of a relationship—that is fundamental to a creative marriage and home.

At a high school conference on preparation for marriage, someone asked, "Who gives the orders around the house?" While that was a rhetorical question in the mind of every listening married man, it was an important question for the young people involved in the discussion group. It was even more important to tell them that in the kind of a home they want no orders are to be given. Of course there will be conclusions reached by various degrees of duress, I suppose, but no orders. For in a creative and stable home, co-operation rules over all. Let pride loose in a marriage, and it is weakened at once. Let pride loose in a home, and sooner or later pieces of that home will be found all along the highway of life. Humility insists upon a proper regard for the right of the other to be heard and heeded in any proposition which involves mutual effort. The fact that so many of our marriages get into difficulty indicates that we have a long way to go in mastering the meaning of humility in the realm of personal relationships.

V

If we see ourselves, even dimly, against the vast backdrop of God's will for us, for other people, for all mankind, no one will need to tell us not to rush for the seats of honor in the kingdom of God. For we will know beyond all doubt that we are not fit to be there at all. We will be deeply grateful to be there and glad to let the master of the feast seat us according to whatever merit or worth he thinks we may have. God himself will make all this plain to us as we stand in His presence.

To stand in that presence is to see ourselves as a part of a will that involves all men, not one more and not one less than another. Once we see ourselves in that perspective, pride dies. We stand on the plane of unforced and unquestioned equality with all men everywhere and are grateful to God for it.

No matter how much we may love ourselves or our work or our church or our country or our way of life, once we have seen ourselves in the presence of the Master of the feast in the kingdom of God, we shall not ask for seats of honor. We will be content with whatever seats He indicates. Humility means the willingness to let God be God, to let Him put us in our proper place in His kingdom, and be glad for it whatever it is. And with that spiritual acceptance of God as God, there will be a new birth of love for Him and confidence in Him.

John Woolman once declared that a new life began for him when he determined to place his whole trust in God. To place our whole trust in God as the Master of the feast, the Host, the One who will put us in our proper place, is to rescue us forever from the temptation to put other people in their place; we are willing to leave that to God. This is the foundation of Christian ethics and Christian living. It is fundamental to every Christian relationship. It is a hard lesson, but well worth the learning.

17. Your Sins Are Forgiven!

LUKE 7:36-50

I

The forgiving spirit comes hard, yet it is one of the inescapable essentials of a Christian reaction to the love of God as we see it in Jesus Christ. Many incidents and teachings from the life of our Lord sharpen up this point—none more so than one which revolved around a meal given him by a Pharisee named Simon. So far as we are able to determine, the other guests were probably Pharisees.

Scarcely had the meal begun when a woman came into the room and stood at the feet of the couch on which Jesus was reclining. Though she took the position traditionally assumed by the servant of an honored and wealthy person, she was no servant. An early scholar has put it accurately, though bluntly, "The woman was a sinner." She had planned to bathe his feet with ointment, as was the custom of the day, but her emotions got out of hand and tears took the place of oil. She dried his feet with her hair "as an expression of homage, of reverence and love, such as would naturally arise out of the deepest and truest feelings of the human heart."

Simon the host was critical both of the woman's presence and behavior and of Jesus' acceptance of her. To Simon, she was no beggar seeking food to which she was entitled by custom. She was a sinner intruding herself among his guests and giving way to a disgusting display of emotionalism. Simon could not understand why Jesus did not order her to leave at once—which was his duty if he did not want her there. Jesus read Simon's thoughts right—and told him the parable of two debtors.

A creditor had two debtors; one owing him one hundred dollars, the

143

other ten dollars. Since neither could pay, he forgave both. Jesus asked, "Which one would love him more?" Simon answered, somewhat dubiously, "The one, I suppose, to whom he forgave more." Jesus agreed, then applied it to the woman's presence. "What she does springs from the depths of her love because her many sins have been forgiven. She does all she can—she must do all she can—to try to express her love, gratitude, and joy." Then he sharpened it up, saying, "Simon, you have been forgiven little, therefore you love little. The emotions and the deeds of love seem strange to you because you are a stranger to the source from which they spring."

Turning to the woman, knowing all were listening intently, he said, "Your sins are forgiven. Your faith has saved you; go in peace."

II

The main figures in the story are still with us—at least, the woman and Simon—and, let us hope, something of the spirit of Jesus.

The woman, of course, is the point of challenge in the story. The Greek name given her implies that she was a person of bad character, probably a prostitute. She was widely known and properly shunned by respectable people. How, when, and where it had happened, we do not know, but she had come under the spell of our Lord and had turned from her evil ways, trusting in his word of forgiveness. What he had promised—that the weight of her sins would be lifted—had actually happened. She felt free of them. She had a new life to live. She was a new person. Small wonder she sought him out, hoping to express her gratitude for the cleansing power of the love of God that had come to her through him.

Now about Simon—there's no point making him out a villain. At least, he was willing to have Jesus in his house and at his table with friends. His attitude toward the woman was approved by his friends. They held to the ancient notion that evil is contagious, and that a wise man will stay away from sinners. Certainly a man of God, a holy man who valued his holiness, would not risk himself by needless exposure to sin and sinners. The severest indictment we can bring against Simon is to describe his sin. He was a man with his mind all made up, and he did not propose to let anyone change it.

Sometimes, for a fleeting moment, I envy people like Simon; people who somehow manage to live in a neat, tidy little world. I envy them because I covet the peace they seem to enjoy, the poise they seem to have as they move through a troubled world with an untroubled mind.

But only for a moment do I envy them! Think how much of God's unfolding truth they must miss! How much of His thunder and lightning they never hear or see! Simon heard everything Jesus said, but I doubt whether he understood it, let alone believed it. They moved in radically different spiritual and moral worlds; Jesus in one in which the love of God was a great new power in the molding of life and affairs; Simon in a fixed and finished world in which the revelation of God had been reduced to writing and all that was needful was to study the writing and obey its leading.

Looking at the woman of the streets, standing erect in joy and gratitude with a sense of freedom and new life, Jesus cried: "This is of God." Simon looked at the same woman, but he did not see what Jesus saw. Jesus saw—and Simon missed—the living power of God in her joy and peace. Simon believed in God, to be sure—the God of Israel, the Lord of the Covenant, the Lord of history. Jesus believed this, too, but at a much deeper level. He believed in God as the Father of this needy woman—One whose love had flowed through her and about her, cleansing her from sin.

Simon wrote the woman off as lost. Jesus saw in her a redeemed person, one in whom the power of the love of God had wrought salvation from sin. His confidence in the presence of that power rings through his words, "Your sins are forgiven. Your faith has saved you; go in peace."

III

The longer we reflect on this incident, the richer it will become in permanent meanings for daily life.

Will anyone deny our need for its instruction in the proper approach to one who has sinned? We must learn it if we are to manage the disgust, bitterness, self-righteousness, and pride which rise up to cripple and blind us as we approach those who, like the woman in the story, have set themselves outside the limits of confidence and respect. Eye them with disgust, approach them with a holier-than-thou attitude, as Simon did, and we deny rather than proclaim our faith in the love of God.

A sinner—I care not what the sin—is a child of God who stands in special need of a new relationship with God and man, and we are called to help him find it. See him and ourselves in this perspective and, of a sudden, the sinner becomes a neighbor, a friend, one to whom we turn in honest concern and affection—as sincere disciples of our Lord would do.

Still another meaning of the story haunts us: *Love is the most powerful force on earth*. It can cast out fear. It can overcome anger and hatred. It can cleanse people like us from sin. Love can do all these impossible things because it is of God; It is the truest carrier of His power and will. "Love is of God," cries the New Testament. And we feel the power of this faith in our Lord's approach to the sinful woman. The love of God had entered into her life and swept it clean of the Devil that had been driving her. The love of God had brought her a new sense of the dignity, worth, and purity of her life in God's sight— and she became a different person because of this experience.

Jesus had the eyes to see it. He believed in the power of God's love, having felt it himself. He knew it could do what, plainly, it had done in this woman. He rejoiced with her in her new life, a gift of God's love to her. He was not indulging in a sentimental gesture; he was stating a fact when he said, "Your sins are forgiven. Your faith has saved you; go in peace."

IV

Our Lord tried to reach Simon by making his point another way: "With what measure ye mete, it shall be measured to you again." Which is a way of saying that we actually determine how much God can do for us. Not how much He *wants* to do, but how much He *can* do. If our love for Him is little, our faith will be weak. And if love and faith are small, the influence of His love will be small. I do not think we are putting it too crudely to suggest that love and faith are the doors through which the love of God enters our lives—and their size determines the amount and the extent of its influence.

Simon and his comrades either missed this point or did not believe it. They thought the power of God came to those who studied and kept the written law. The good life, to their way of thinking, was one which conformed to the traditions of their faith. They honored the men who kept the law; they cast out the ones who did not. This, to them, was the simple rule of righteousness and faith. Like one of the

Psalmists, they had no hesitation in crying, "I hate those who hate Thy law."

Let us not make Simon's mistake and judge him too harshly though. His, I suppose, is the way we usually do things; honor those who do what they are supposed to do and turn our backs on those who do not.

All Christians need to say, and it is more than enough, is that we ought to love God as He loves us; we ought to honor His love more than we honor our customs and conventions when there is conflict between the two. His love can overcome any sin that is brought to Him in love and faith. And we ought to be among those who not only turn to Him in love for the cleansing of our own life; we ought, also, to be witnesses of this to others. Yet only as we love Him utterly can His love become the dominant factor in our lives.

It is at this point that the realism of the New Testament becomes terrifyingly plain. We cannot honor and honestly love God unless we love our fellow men. Are you jarred, as I confess I always am, when you read, "If any one says, I love God, and hates his brother, he is a liar; for he who does not love his brother whom he has seen, cannot love God whom he has not seen. And this commandment we have from him, that he who loves God should love his brother also" (I John 4:20-21). This is much too plain for comfort.

There is no evidence that the Great Teacher was able to open Simon's eyes to this truth. Simon's species did not die with him. He lives on in us and all around us. We continue to try the impossible—to hate man and to love God. We continue to work the works of hate rather than the works of love, and wonder why it is we are children of hatred and conflict ourselves. We continue to have small doors of love and faith and, in consequence, feel only the feeblest impulse of God's mighty love in our own lives. We are like a point on a tidal river so far from the ocean that mighty tides produce only the slightest rise and fall in the water level. Just so, by our own choice, we are so far removed from the full meaning of God's love that we feel only the slightest pulsations of it—enough to know that it is there, but not enough to be controlled by its redemptive and recreative power.

V

Our Lord had no illusions about the difficulty of the task he was giving his disciples when he said, "By this shall all men know that ye are my disciples, that ye love one another"; when he made mutual forgiveness an integral part of our fellowship in the kingdom of God, when he prayed and asked his disciples to pray, "Forgive us our trespasses as we forgive those that trespass against us."

Think about it for a moment: Could it be otherwise? God neither can nor will transform our lives by love unless we are willing that they should be transformed. He cannot forgive us unless we are able to forgive others. Only as we are forgiving in spirit can we be forgiven by His Holy Spirit. Only as the forgiving spirit becomes our spirit can the consciousness of being forgiven by God become a living reality in our own life.

And Jesus pushes the point home hard with his insistence that men who would find peace with God must be willing to seek peace with their brethren. I know of no saying of his that makes the altar of our churches more austere than this: "If you are offering your gift at the altar, and there remember that your brother has something against you, leave your gift there before the altar and go; first be reconciled to your brother, and then come and offer your gift" (Matt. 5:23-24). Our Lord will not let us separate man and God from each other in order that we may love and adore the one and hate and kill the other. He insists that these are inseparable ideas in great religious living.

For him, there is no such thing as a purely human relationship. In dealing with each other, we also deal with God. It is impossible for a man who refuses to forgive his brother to be forgiven by God. When we refuse to another the greatest of Christian gifts—the gift of forgiving love—we deny ourselves the gift all men seek: The experience of the forgiving love of God. Religion and life, faith and works, the sanctuary and the home, the school, and the market place are not separate compartments in which we can indulge in love in some and hate in others. They are so intertwined with each other that love, to be genuine in any of them, must pervade all of them. Or, conversely, if hate has a firm rootage in some of them, it will find its way in some form or other to all. Sensing this profound unity in life, Jesus said, "Forgive us our trespasses as we forgive those who trespass against us." And he warned his followers, "For if you forgive them their trespasses, your heavenly Father also will forgive you; but if you do not forgive men their trespasses, neither will your Father forgive your trespasses."

Against the background of this whole pattern of thought, forgiving love makes sense.

VI

Let no Christian beg off from accepting the discipline of forgiving love by saying that it cannot operate in actual living. I have seen it at work time and time again, and I know it can help persons neither better nor wiser than ordinary folk.

I think of a family in the Mount Vernon Place Methodist Church in Baltimore who had lost their only son during World War II. The day that war ended we had a service of solemn rejoicing in the church, and afterward, instead of joining the throngs on the street, I went to the home of this family and sat in the garden with them. We heard the noise of rejoicing swell up from the heart of the great city, and we, too, were glad the war was over. But in the quiet of the garden, our thoughts were on other things. Finally, as if speaking to herself, the mother said, "I don't hate anyone. I just can't bear to think of adding anything more to the grief of the world."

When in Japan visiting colleges and seminaries, I met a young man who had just returned from a student work camp in the Philippines. He told how he had been exposed for the first time to the murderous hatred of the Filipinos for the Japanese. When the airplane flying him from Japan landed in Manila, he was taken almost at once to the bronze statue of the beheaded woman which commemorated the savagery of the military rule of the Japanese army. He was stunned, and wished he could go home. His hosts for the summer were a Filipino family who had lost two sons in the fighting. The Japanese student said, "These good Christian folk took me in as one of them. I found peace in their home."

Sometimes I hear it said that if we practice forgiving love, we will be a doormat for the scoundrels of the world. Look at these incidents again. Now let me ask whether in your judgment people who can do things like these are weak? Rather, are they not the fairest fruit of the Christian ethic? Do they not know and exhibit the kind of strength that we need desperately these days?

If we can substitute forgiving love for hatred, as they did, we can do anything! And we are called upon to do just that: To overcome hatred with love, by practicing forgiving love ourselves to know the power of the forgiving love of God. This is the Christian gospel, the Christian mission in the world where there is so much hatred, so little love; so much darkness, so little light. It is a gospel of peace—peace through love and forgiveness; peace with ourselves, peace with each other, and peace with God.

18. The God of the Lost

I

The Christian faith has always been concerned for the salvation of the individual and society alike. How could it be otherwise—if we honor the lead of our Lord? He defined the purpose of his life in these terms: "I have come to seek and to save that which is lost." And he spells out the meaning of this with beauty and power in three well-known parables: the lost sheep, the lost coin, and the lost son, better known as the prodigal son.

C. G. Montefiore, one of the great scholars of Judaism, finds the novelty of Jesus' teaching in this group of stories:

The virtues of repentance are gloriously praised in the Rabbinical literature, but this direct search for, and appeal to, the sinner, are new and moving notes of high import and significance. The good shepherd who searches for the lost sheep, and reclaims it and rejoices over it, is a new figure, which has never ceased to play its great part in the moral and religious development of the world.[1]

The parables do present a new conception of God—"*The God of the lost*." They tell of the seeking love of God which will not give up anyone for lost.

One of the most influential pictures in my boyhood home was a vivid depiction of the good shepherd seeking the one lost sheep. While I am sure it would not rank as great art, it gave at least one of its viewers an unforgettable picture of the seeking love of God which will not rest until it has reclaimed all its lost children.

Several things about this parable of the good shepherd continue to impress me mightily. For one thing, the shepherd was not a prudent man, i.e., he did not "play percentages." Certainly a prudent man would have been glad to settle for the "ninety and nine" who were safe and not risk his life in an idealistic effort to find the foolish one that had strayed away. But he must not have thought prudence a primary virtue. Imprudent or not, he was "the good shepherd" who felt an unshakable duty to take care of all his flock to the very limit of his concern and energy. And he kept at it until he found the one lost lamb and brought it back to the safety of the fold.

The parables make two points that set the bells of earth and heaven ringing: (1) man is a creature of absolute worth in the sight of God; (2) God seeks all men through love and will never give up until He finds them. Obviously, these are more than stern indictments of the scribes and the Pharisees who were falling down on the job of being shepherds of the lost sheep of Israel; they are "marching orders" for his disciples in all generations. Jesus defined both his own life and ministry and that of his disciples when he insisted, "I have come to seek and to save that which is lost."

Here in a dozen words is our most reliable understanding of what salvation means to the Christian. It is that moment and experience wherein the seeking love of God and the needy life of man meet and merge. When this happens, we are "found," which means that our lives have a new center of loyalty and love, that we are at home with God and man again, gaining confidence in ourselves and our work.

It is the permanent glory of Jesus Christ—and the Christian faith at its best—that he regarded himself as the one through whom the saving love of God becomes a living reality in the lives of men. He identified himself with all when he said that he had come to seek and to save the lost. For he tried and continues to try to get us to see that we can accept by faith the outstretched hand of God and be saved thereby, can be restored to a creative personal relationship with God and man. Though subsequent generations of Christians have tried to explain the why and how of its many ways, all agree that both lostness and salvation are facts of and in human life and experience.

II

Far from being the concern of the Christian faith alone, salvation is the central concern of the great religions of the world. This was made abundantly clear in the series of splendid interpretations given us by

Life magazine a number of years ago and published later in book form as *The World's Great Religions.* Without exception, these are ways in which men who feel themselves lost believe they have recovered a sense of belonging to the deep purposes of the world in which we live. The quest for salvation, then, is not only one of the oldest, but it continues to be one of the most universal and urgent concerns of men. Notions of what it means and how to achieve it may and will vary widely, but the longing and the need for it, the passionate belief in it, the endless variations in man's search for it—these are constants in human experience.

Sometimes we find expressions of the quest for salvation in unexpected places. On Febraury 24, 1949, the sedate columns of the *New York Times* carried this interesting and unusual paragraph:

What must we do to be saved? In a thousand forms—and with a thousand answers—that is still man's leading and most tormenting soliloquy. Man wants the good life, the full life, and as much security as possible this side of paradise. No jesting Pilate, he will stay for the answers that all the Pilates can offer him in his wonderously dogged pursuit of peace and happiness.

Ask any thoughtful man, "What must we do to be saved?" And if he will consider the question at all, he will wind up somewhere in the field of religion, talking about faith in God and man.

One of the reasons we can never treat the Bible as merely "great literature" (which it surely is) is the passionate sincerity of its concern for salvation. The Bible is the most relevant book in our world because we continue to get lost and we continue to need salvation in every important sense of these ancient terms.

William Ernest Hocking once described the lost soul as a person who had lost the confidence and the power of belief in his fellows and in the universe. One of my beloved teachers, Arthur E. Holt, said, "A man is lost when he cannot define his present or plan his future." Not only have I felt that kind of lostness myself many times, but I have seen many others lost in exactly the same sense.

Lost sometimes in the fog of fear, anxiety, and worry, they grope frantically, even desperately, for a sure way to the level of clear vision. Lost sometimes in the jungles of passion, hatred, and vengeance, they are unable to see men truly or to judge events fairly, and they react in spasms of animal fury. Lost sometimes in the vast confusion of our time which stretches in all directions like a trackless Sahara, they strike out blindly, futilely, in any direction just to keep going. Lost sometimes when an illness like drunkenness fastens itself upon them, stripping them of confidence and self-respect, they have neither the courage nor the stamina to face the problems and reverses that must be faced in daily living. Lost sometimes because they do not learn how to manage defeat and disappointment, and thus find themselves in periodic and full retreat from the inevitable encounters of life. Lost, in summary, in these and many other ways because in a precise sense they have lost confident touch with God, with man, with themselves, and are unable to define their present or to plan their future.

Our most discerning writers are well aware of the tragedy of this fact of lostness. Dostoevski could describe it with unparalleled power because for years he, himself, was lost in a mania for gambling that stripped him of morals and dependable character. Finally he hit bottom when he stole his sick wife's clothing, pawned it, and then lost the money at the wheel. Utterly destitute of both money and self-respect, he could only creep home, a lost soul, and seek his wife's forgiveness.

The young German soldier in Erich Maria Remarque's great novel, *All Quiet on the Western Front,* turns away from the chaos of the battle-field so symbolic of the confusion of his generation, with the prophetic words, "I—I think we are lost." It is not hard for me to realize that a generation believing this was able to and did produce both Adolf Hitler and his many supporters in the Third Reich. Willie, in *Death of a Salesman,* and Blanche, in *Streetcar Named Desire,* and a dozen others are examples of lost souls on the stages of our theaters and in our motion pictures. One of the reasons we go to see them is because we feel, "There, but for the grace of God, am I." And sometimes we are not sure we have the right to say that. For, in our candid moments, we find ourselves saying, "I—I think we are lost."

Some years ago, a panel of scientists and religionists were asked to consider the relationship between science and religion. The four scientists in the group, though proud of the achievements of science, were sobered instantly by the question whether science, of itself, could guide mankind to a stabler future. As if animated by a single impulse, each reached for the microphone and asked to answer. Their answers

THE GOD OF THE LOST

added up to this: Science alone will wreck the world. Religion through faith in God must show the way or we are lost.

Nor is the matter of lostness confined to individuals alone. The fact that one marriage in every three now ends in divorce is a reminder that great relationships, like individuals, can get lost. The normal creative unfolding of the shared life so radiantly expectant in the moment of marriage can be distorted, arrested, or wholly blocked by any one of a long series of events and developments. But, whatever the active cause, the result is the same—the promise of the shared life is blighted and the individual components of it go through the scarring process of separating themselves from each other and trying to start living a wholly different kind of life. When a marriage reaches that point, it is a "lost" relationship in a most exact sense.

The same sort of "lostness" can overtake other great relationships in life, whether a partnership in business, or citizenship in a country, or membership in a church. Will anyone deny that a very dangerous kind of lostness has overtaken Western civilization? Statesmen, political leaders, and thoughtful students are appalled at the precarious character of the "balance of terror" or the "stalemate of fears" in which we live. A distinguished member of the bar of New York City, John F. Wharton, contributed three articles to the *Saturday Review* which sobered, shocked, and stirred their readers. Beginning with the calm assertion that, "barring a miracle, the United States of America will be devastated by a nuclear war not later than 1970," he continues to enlarge on what he calls "the threat and the promise" of the present situation. While he is sure there is a way out, he is also convinced that the time given us to find it is so perilously short as to demand a rebirth of idealistic endeavor on the part of individuals and groups alike.

And as we totter on the brink of the precipice of what will be the final war in the history of mankind, unless we are wholly insensitive to anything deeper than the jingoistic pride which runs through all right-wing pronouncements that cry for victory at any cost, we will have that sickening, sinking sensation which caused the young soldier to whisper, "I—I think we are lost." Not long ago, a thoughtful friend shocked me by saying, quite calmly, "I confess I am pleased at the prospect of history's end. It's been a bum show from the beginning."

This multiple experience of being lost, in whatever form we may encounter it, is no stranger in the household of religious faith. In fact, it is the most persistent caller known there,—and none is more welcome —for religion tries to take hold of a man or of a society precisely at that point to help him find himself and his way in the sure will of God. No complacency, let alone smugness, is intended in the assertion that the Christian faith has met and mastered, in principle at least, and in life in fact, every known form of lostness which has beset mankind. We cannot say that salvation is inevitable or that it is easy, but we can and do say that it is possible, that it has been made possible through the life and teachings of Jesus Christ—which is why we call him our Saviour and the Christian faith the gospel of salvation.

III

If we are going to be true to him, we shall not want to ignore or play down the two lessons he was driving home in the parables of the lost:

1. Man is a creature of absolute worth in the sight of God—and we just don't play percentages with him! Talk about the spiritual under-girding of a human being or a democracy which is based upon faith in human beings—there we have it!

And the second emphasis adds strength to it:

2. God seeks all men through love *and never gives up on any man.*

Is it possible to say more plainly than this, why the Christian Church will not—because she cannot—settle for less than all? We are not interested in a world order in which one nation or one way of life survives at the expense of others; nor are we interested in a world where one human being survives at the expense of another. The Great Commission of our faith was not the end product of a week's deliberation by a committee of prudent men seeking a respectable and safe course of action for the church. It sprang from the heart of One who is the good shepherd of all—and it struck fire in the hearts of the men and women like ourselves who rose from Pentecost, faced outward from the center, and then went to the ends of the world as servants of the seeking God.

A vital church is a seeking church. We cannot serve the God of the lost unless we are willing to seek them out wherever they are and reclaim them no matter who they are. The method of doing this may and will vary from generation to generation, but the need to do it is constant. This is the first as well as the final argument for the missionary activities of the Christian Church. To those who bid us stay at home and take care of the needs close at hand, we say we must be loyal to the God who seeks to reclaim all His children. Of course we have a man-sized job at home—no one can deny that. But it is only a portion of the problem which is in the spotlight of divine concern. Our full obligation is to be of use wherever we can reach people at the point of their need. Only thus can we be servants of the seeking God.

IV

It is our radiant conviction that Jesus Christ will step to our side in the role of "the Good Shepherd" as we seek to be good shepherds and will help us find our way in the will of God and be our inspiration and guide as we share this faith with others.

Vachel Lindsay put all this and more in four unforgettable lines:

> This is our faith tremendous,—
> Our wild hope, who shall scorn,—
> That in the name of Jesus
> The world shall be reborn![2]

I know how incredible this must seem to those who may have gone through life without paying much attention to the meaning of God. That the God of the universe, of the wheeling planets, of the infinite stretches of the cosmos, that He is concerned about us as the good shepherd is concerned about an individual sheep which had strayed away: "It's too good to be true," men have said for thousands of years. Yet it is true.

We are like sailors on one of the old sailing vessels that had been blown off her course along the coast of South America. The crew had lost all sense of time and place. Their water was running low and they were anxiously hoping for some port. Spying another vessel early one morning, they signaled for water. The answer came back, "Let down your buckets. You're in the mouth of the Amazon River. There's fresh water all around."

Are we looking for the spiritual foundation for the good life and the good society? It is all around us!

Are we looking for the turning point in our flight from fear, loneliness, and confusion? This is it.

Are we looking for a positive approach to the meaning of life, duty, and work? Then let us take our stand here, and about face.

Are we looking for a new sense of the worth of the church? What more can we ask than this gospel of the seeking of God who reaches out for any and all of us?

To one and all and to none more than to ourselves, we say: "Salvation is possible—through the grace of the God of the lost and our faith in Him."

19. Honored by God

MATTHEW 20:20-28; LUKE 18:9-14

I

The desire for recognition is both human and universal. If we cannot get it one way, we seek it another. If we cannot achieve it by fair means, we are not averse to using foul means. There is nothing evil in this desire until and unless the recognition we seek is separated from honest worth. No right-thinking person would begrudge Albert Schweitzer, for example, a place of honor in any gathering of the distinguished citizens of the world. When the World Council of Churches held its Second Assembly in Evanston in 1954, John R. Mott was given a seat of honor at all services in recognition of a lifetime of work to bring churches together. Men like these grace seats of honor because they have earned them. But it is noteworthy that such men do not seek them; rather they shun them so steadily that it is necessary to all but force them to occupy them. Humility is usually a distinguishing mark of great spirits. And humility is a hard quality to capture.

Upon two occasions Jesus was confronted by people who, lacking in humility, sought seats of honor.

Matthew tells of the time when the aggressive mother of two of his disciples put a straight request to him that he promise that "these two sons of mine may sit, one at your right hand and one at your left, in your kingdom" (Matt. 20:21). Jesus dealt kindly with her. Like every other mother, she saw her sons' ability and worth through the haze of her great love for them. Jesus told her that he could make no such promise since God himself would indicate who would deserve to sit in the seats of honor in the kingdom.

This very human incident from the life of the little company of disciples is of a piece with the familiar story of the Pharisee and the publican who had come to the Temple to pray (Luke 18:9-14). Here, surely, is an etching on the conscience of man of the right and wrong ways to look toward God.

Can anyone forget the Pharisee, who, honestly feeling he had kept the law and was therefore more righteous than other men, could lift his eyes confidently to heaven and thank God he was not like this publican who had not tried to keep God's law at all? Will any deny the existence within himself of the pharisaical spirit which tempts us to set ourselves above others as being better, or more righteous, or more Christian than they?

Can we forget that poor publican who was suddenly aware of his unworthiness? What had he done with his time? How had he become so blinded to the claims of God as to neglect or ignore them? Why, oh why, had he sinned against God so casually and so completely with his life?

No one knows why the publican's little world suddenly caved in on him, but it did, and he was smart enough to know it and honest enough to admit it. To the Temple he went intent on confession and repentance. He was so acutely and personally centered in God that I doubt whether he even knew the Pharisee was at his side. Certainly he did not pray, "I confess I am worse than this Pharisee!" What he did say, and I suspect all he could say, is well known, "God be merciful to me a sinner."

That, said Jesus, is the proper way to approach God—in humility, in complete gratitude for being able to approach Him at all, seeking a renewal of a creative relationship with Him. Men who feel this way are dear to God and will be invited to know the fuller meaning of His love.

There is yet another incident from the New Testament, drawn from real life, of people who want everyone to know when they are on their way to the Temple with a great gift (Mark 12:41-44). As Jesus tells the story, trumpets cleared the way for them to approach the Temple, to enter the gates, and then to stand in marked humility to one side as their servants laid their great contribution before the altar. Then, undoubtedly, they received the cordial thanks and fulsome blessing of the delighted priests who knew that the budget would be balanced if only enough men could be interested in doing this!

Yet as this fanfare was monopolizing the center of the stage, Jesus saw a poor woman approach, hesitate, hastily drop two coins in the box, then leave with no one but himself paying any attention to her. But what attention he gave her! He immortalized her as the spirit of true giving to God: "What she gives comes from her livelihood. She will have less to eat and drink and wear because of what she has given to God." Why did she do it, then, we want to know. Because she had to do it. She had to bring God some token of her love for Him, her joy in His presence, her desire to perpetuate for her children the Temple, the law, and the celebration of His goodness to her and her people.

That spirit, said Jesus, opens wide the gate to the very throne of God. That gift does more to preserve and enrich the worship of God than all the gold and silver proud men in search of a reputation for piety can conceivably heap before the altar.

When what one gives, be it ever so humble, is torn out of the very fabric of the need of his life, through his love for God and joy in His service, that gift goes to the heart of God as no other gift can. Thus the smallest gift, as men reckon worth, can easily be the greatest gift, as God reckons worth. And, lest we forget, the worth of our gift is finally judged by God, not by men!

II

The scene in this drama of humility and gratitude to God shifts a bit —but not much—as we read Paul's letters to the Corinthians. He and other Christians were both appalled and overwhelmed with joy in their calling. They were appalled because they were preaching the gospel to all men: rich and poor; powerful and weak; Jew and Gentile. By what right did they do this? Were they better, or wiser, or more powerful than the ones to whom they were preaching? Obviously not! Something of their confident joy comes ringing through these words of Paul:

For consider your call, brethren; not many of you were wise according to worldly standards, not many were powerful, not many were of noble birth; but God chose what is foolish in the world to shame the wise, God chose what is weak in the world to shame the strong. God chose what is low and despised in the world, even things that are not, to bring to nothing things that are, so that no human being might boast in the presence of God. He is the source of your life in Christ Jesus, whom God made our wisdom, our righteousness and sanctification and redemption; therefore, as it is written, Let him who boasts, boast of the Lord (I Cor. 1:26-31).

The all-important claims in this passage are these: God chose; God calls us; God gives us life; let our rejoicing be not in ourselves but in the God we find in Jesus Christ.

Everywhere in the New Testament we discover this incredulous joy over the fact that God had called them into His service. No matter that it led to privation, hardship, prison, and death. The only thing that mattered was He had opened the door of service, and their joy on entering it knew no bounds. They could not understand why He had opened it to them—the poor, the lowly, the weak, the outcast—but He had, and that was enough to set the joy-bells ringing in them and in the church for all time!

Who were they—these early Christians—who lovingly, humbly called themselves "the people of God"? They were "common people" —that much is clear on every page of the New Testament as well as in every other scrap of evidence we are able to find.

Gibbon, bitterly contemplating the decline and fall of the Roman Empire, gives the Christians the back of his hand in this violent, if classic, judgment: "Christians were almost entirely composed of the dregs of the populace, of peasants and mechanics, of boys and women, of beggars and slaves." Probably the most reliable estimate from the historians is that of Shirley Jackson Case: Christianity was composed of "the working class and small tradesmen; the majority were slaves, common laborers and people without recognized social status."

Any way you want to look at it, no one joined the early Christian church for social, economic, or political recognition. It made its way most rapidly in the lowest social stratum of that day, yet it could not be confined to that group. It burst upward and outward early and with amazing rapidity. Soon after the learned Celsus attacked Christianity, equally learned men like Clement of Alexandria and Origen rose to the defense. Christian thinkers captured school after school in one great center after another until a literal chain of them girdled the eastern end of the Mediterranean. Officials might imprison Peter, Paul, and other Apostles, but they could not keep the prisoners from converting their jailers. Before long we hear of Christians in high office and even in the imperial household.

The matter, I suspect, can be reduced to some such statement as this: Christianity grew because it had the common touch. It gave men a status before God that no human power could either give or take away.

Hence it was prized by kings and subjects, masters and slaves, rich and poor alike.

The most eloquent evidence of the magic of the common touch of the early church is the very language of the New Testament itself. For centuries Christian scholars were puzzled by the peculiar kind of Greek found in the New Testament. It was different from the classical Greek used by Plato and Aristotle. In fact, it was so utterly unlike any other known form that slightly irreverent scholars sometimes called it "Holy Ghost Greek." The mystery began to lift about seventy years ago with the discovery in the sands of Egypt of literally thousands of records and letters from the first century. All were written in the language used by ordinary people in daily life. Among them were a housekeeper's record of food purchased for slaves; a soldier's letter home asking his parents to send him extra clothing—and countless other items of similar trivial but human nature. The language of these letters and records was the "unstilted language of the people." And it is exactly the same language used in the New Testament. Adolf Deissmann, the scholar who did so much to interpret the meaning of this discovery, says, "The gospel, because it was the message of God to humanity, could only reveal itself in the simplest of garments." And he puts professors and theologians and their technical jargon in place with the observation that Jesus' "words remain in the minds and souls of simple men, who had never been burdened with learned ballast. In the gospel simple, great lines join heaven and earth, powerful trumpet sounds arouse the conscience, the everyday facts of human life are the revelation of the eternal. . . . Because the Apostles spoke the peoples' languages, the gospel could go among the masses, could start a mission, and could wander from coast to coast." This New Testament that we handle daily, "this simple book, with its carpenter's and tent-maker's language, was a book for all, and it could resound, unadulterated, to humanity in all centuries, the message of the gospel which had moved men in a small corner of the Mediterranean world."[1]

The powerful church in this or any other age is a fellowship of ordinary people made extraordinary by their faith in, and joy over, the love of God which comes to them in Jesus Christ. From this faith and joy comes the kind of service that has taken the Christian witness to the ends of the earth.

III

Considerations like these provide, as it were, a brightly lighted stage on which much of our life passes in swift review. And what we see there will remind some of us of an incident in Dick Sheppard's *Poems of the Padre*—poems based on his experiences as a chaplain in the British army in World War I. He tells of the Tommy who was killed in battle and was on his way to final Judgment. Understandably alarmed at what he faced, he was thinking out as good a case for himself as he could. He had decided to rest his plea on the grounds that he was not much worse than anyone else and on that basis deserved some consideration. Came the climatic moment, and he stood before Jesus Christ and began his plea. But as he started to talk, he saw in the eyes of the Master, as on a gigantic stage, all that he had ever been and done. The Tommy's plea faded away as he watched the sorry procession. Finally, he blurted out, "Please, Lord, can't I go to Hell!"

Is it not true that we are all but driven into becoming a race of pushers, climbers, wire-pullers, influence peddlers, status-seekers? Do you ever hear anyone speaking about the ideal of growing in wisdom and stature and in favor with God and man? Now it is how to get ahead, whether by merit or pull, but how to get ahead at all costs. We are in danger of turning into a generation of publicity hounds. We sacrifice poise to push; we lay integrity, honor, friendship, health, and sometimes our families on the altar of what William James once bitingly called "the bitch-goddess of success." It's "rush, hurry, push, shove, trample, be at the right place at the right time to be seen by the right people," until our very soul seems spun out of us by the whirling pace.

We are all involved in this sort of pressure to some extent. I think of the young couple who moved to Evanston, Illinois, from the South. Soon after they joined our church, I found her almost in tears because, she said, "I am getting so I feel ashamed because I am not doing half a dozen different things." Recently a brilliant young executive in one of the radio companies quit his job because, he said, "It isn't worth it to live under that kind of pressure." It is one thing—and commendable —to have the ambition to be in a post where one's abilities and interests are fully used. It is quite another thing to seek that post without being ready for it, without belonging there through merit. Seats of honor are chairs of torture to those who do not belong there. Some of the unhappiest people I know are those who have wormed their way into positions of responsibility they are incapable of handling. Fear of failure haunts them every waking moment and produces marked distortions in their lives and relationships.

I am tempted to say that people like these are more to be pitied because they are much unhappier than those who sit in the lower seat of recognition and are disappointed because their merit is not fully appreciated.

What I am saying will be misunderstood completely if it is taken as counsel to "lie low, don't try to get ahead, give up all ambition, take whatever life dishes out." I do not mean that at all. The desire for recognition, the desire to serve to the full extent of one's ability, is an essential part of any normal personality. It becomes a problem only when it gets separated from merit, on the one hand, and, on the other, from the realization that others in position of responsibility may not agree with our valuation of ourselves. And when this happens, we need to be ready to accept their judgment without bitterness.

The spirit that insists on seats of honor and recognition at all costs is its own greatest problem. It is usually a proud, jealous, suspicious quarrelsome spirit. It is not blessed with laudable self-confidence; it is cursed with the consuming ambition. The man who drives is usually one who is driven. And the man whose very life depends upon being given a seat of honor on the right or left hand of the central person will know neither peace nor poise of mind or spirit even if he should be given so eminent a seat. For they must be always on guard against the fear that there will be those around seeking to displace them! The only proper approach to this desire for recognition and preferment in life, is, as Jesus said, to accept and rejoice in the fact that our Creator and Companion will reward us according to our merits and do so in the terms of the work He gives us to do.

Years ago Bishop Charles Wesley Flint presided over the Baltimore Methodist Conference when it was meeting in the Mount Vernon Place Methodist Church in Baltimore. He was unruffled and poised in the hubbub of the proceedings. When I commented on it he said, "Well, I do not have to do it alone. In fact, I do only a small part of the work that needs to be done here. God does most of it, and I try to find out how to fit in with what He is doing."

Such a person will not ask for a seat of honor; it will be enough for him to be in the same room with the Master and to serve Him in all humility. Such a one can face success with humility, believing that under God he will be able to bear the responsibilities that come with it. He can face disappointment and failure without losing heart because he believes, under God, he will find the strength to begin again and keep at the work until he wins some measure of success. The secret of the successful Christian life lies somewhere in the area of learning how to walk humbly through each day with the joyful confidence that we are the guests of God and that there is a place for us and what we can do in His holy will for all mankind.

The religious imagery of this may well seem awkward to some. Should this be so, let us not discard the essential truth, but restate it in more congenial language. For it is true, no matter how you say it, that "every one who exalts himself will be humbled, and he who humbles himself will be exalted." God himself will see to that!

20. The Generosity of God

MATTHEW 20:1-16

I

Our reluctance to take seriously what Jesus teaches is an old failing of all who profess to listen to him. If what he says does not fit into our preconceived patterns of how things ought to be, we turn away from him, seeking another who will say what we want to hear. If what he urges on us stretches the horizons of our minds and souls beyond endurance, we expel his teachings and settle back into our tight, cozy, little cocoonlike worlds from which we propose never to emerge. But when we do this, we not only deny him, we deny ourselves fulfillment through him.

One of our Lord's parables illustrates both our need for him and our reluctance to hear him.

II

It came during the final phase of his public ministry when the long shadows pointing toward Calvary were beginning to disturb the disciples. Intimations of defeated dreams and fading hopes for a great popular following met them daily. The religious leaders of Palestine were neither going to hear him out nor follow his leadership. The powerful Temple party—holders of such political power as Rome allowed the Jews—were openly suspicious of his every word and move. Even earnest men, like the rich young ruler, found his advice too hard to take. The common people may have heard him gladly, but there was little evidence that they were going to do much more than just that—hear him! The disciples had begun to feel terribly alone in this great venture of faith in following him. Humanly and quite understandably, they sought assurance that they had been right in following him. It was then he fashioned the parable of the laborers in the vineyard.

The owner of the vineyard needed day laborers. He went to the market place at sunup and hired some men to work that day for the equivalent of a dollar apiece. The worker's day then was no eight-hour affair; it ran from sunup until the stars were clearly visible—usually twelve to fifteen hours. Later in the day—at 9:00 A.M.—the owner hired more workers, saying he would give them what was right. Again at twelve and at three and even as late as five o'clock, he hired still more workers. When the day was over, the ones hired last were paid first and received the same wages as those who had gone to work at sunrise. The all-day laborers objected, thinking they deserved more for the extra hours they had worked.

No sensible man can deny two things: (1) from where they stood, they had a good case for more money; (2) the owner had lived up to his agreement with them. They had received the wages promised when they took the job. They knew it—and the owner knew it, too. His integrity in the sense of keeping his word was not questioned. They felt that he had permitted his generosity, goodness, and sympathy to sway his calculation of what was due the late arrivals on the job. Like the elder brother in the parable of the prodigal son, they felt that their hard work had been slighted. If they were aroused by what they considered the injustice of paying men who had worked three hours the same wage as those who had worked fourteen hours, the owner was aroused by their accusations that he was unfair. He paid them their wage and sent them on their way, asking, "Do you begrudge my generosity?"

We shall want to keep our eye on that word "generosity" if we are to grasp the intent of the parable. For whatever else the parable is, it most assuredly is not a blueprint for negotiating a wage contract between owner and management today. Nor was it ever intended to serve this purpose. What purpose, then, did it serve?

One scholar suggests that it fits in with the desire of the Gospel of Matthew "to show that those who have been meagerly rewarded in this age will be compensated in the age to come, but the actual effect is to intimate that God deals with all men more generously than they deserve." The parable should warn us to be prepared for the fact we discover on every page of the New Testament: There is a vast difference between the standards of men and the standard of God; between the standards with which we are familiar and the standard of His kingdom.

Jesus places in unforgettable words the simple fact that God's love is always a determining factor in His justice; that, in God, justice and love are never separated. Man may separate them, but God never does. Thus what God gives us should better be regarded as reward than wage, more an expression of His love than of our desserts.

Our great students of the human spirit would agree that Jesus exposed one of our deepest needs at this point. When Polonius promises to treat the players according to their desserts, Hamlet objects: "God's bodikins, man, much better; use every man after his dessert, and who should 'scape whipping? Use them after your own honour and dignity; the less they deserve, the more merit is in your bounty."[1] And Joseph Conrad wrote in *The Life Beyond*, "What humanity needs is not the promise of scientific immortality, but compassionate pity in this life and infinite mercy in the Day of Judgment." Jesus would assure Conrad, "We have the love of God in this life, in whatever judgment God pronounces upon it, and in whatever life lies beyond the portals of death."

III

Jesus is saying that the rewards of God as given to men are not arbitrary, except as love and generosity always seem arbitrary by human standards of justice. And he was saying it to all of us who instinctively agree with the complaints of the ones who had worked all day in the vineyard. They were saying, in effect, "Now, if I were running this business, here's how I'd do it. I'd see to it that every man was paid according to a strict scale; so much an hour; so many hours, so much money. That is the only fair and just way to do it. Give a man what he earns by his labors—not a cent more. Give him his just desserts—not an ounce more. Business is business, you know."

Yet this line of reasoning is becoming more and more suspect even in business circles these days. We are beginning to realize that justice is more than a sliderule application of some known law.

Shakespeare put it as neatly as any writer outside the New Testament in his *Merchant of Venice*. When Shylock comes into the court of law demanding justice, in quest of his pound of flesh, Portia grants the validity of his claim, yet urges on him the utter injustice and inadequacy of it. She reminds him that "mercy is above this sceptred sway" of earthly power; that mercy is

> . . . An attribute to God, himself:
> And earthly power doth then show likest God's
> When mercy seasons justice.

She continues:

> Though justice be thy plea, consider this,
> That in the course of justice none of us
> Should see salvation; we do pray for mercy;
> And that same prayer doth teach us all to render
> The deeds of mercy.[2]

We are beginning to realize that "justice is something less than justice unless it is something more." Granted at once, we need law and rules and contracts and all sorts of precisely written technical agreements in order to keep a society together. Granted, further, that without such laws, we would probably be stripped of our rights and freedom in short order. But is it not equally clear that the man who stands on the letter of that law is in danger of doing violence to the spirit of it? Is not the law made to serve life, not life the law?

If that is true in our dealings with each other, how much truer must it be in the kingdom of God? The rules there are God's rules, not ours, expressing not what we would do if we were God (terrible thought!) but what God in His love wants done. On peril of losing our faith, we must resist the temptation to drag God down to our level rather than try to lift ourselves to the level of His will for us. We must resist the temptation to downgrade the kingdom of God until it becomes life as we want it. Rather we must try to upgrade life as we live it until it is life as God wills it.

God's new world has rules, right enough. Read the Sermon on the Mount again if you doubt it! There we have the most compact statement ever made of what is expected of those who actually want to live as God would have them live, who would like to enter the kingdom of God *now*—not by dying, but by living accordingly to His will.

Seeking to interpret God's will to all men, Jesus never lets his listeners forget that *the love of God* undergirds everything God purposes or does for all men. In this parable, he throws light on some of the things this means. God calls some to work early and some late. When the day is done, he rewards them because they have worked, not because of what they have done. Because they heard His call when it came and responded to it by working to the end of the day, the reward of His love was the same for all.

IV

We need to let the meaning of that seep into the very marrow of our souls! It would do more than anything else to answer some questions before they are asked, and it would put all questions about the purpose of life in a radically different perspective.

Why has God given such varied gifts to us, we want to know? To some of us, He has given good health and abounding energies, to others moderate health and fewer energies; to some poor health and very few energies. Why the difference? Well, no man knows—and Jesus did not attempt an answer. But he did say that we should devote all our energies, whether many or few, to His service. God does not expect one to pretend he is another in this matter, but He does expect us to respond to His call with all He has given us.

Some of us have been raised in Christian homes and cannot recall a time when reverence for God and Christ, and respect for the church and the Bible were not a part of our heritage. While faith has not been exactly easy for us, at least it has seemed a normal reaction to life.

Others of us have come from homes that paid only fitful attention to the divine dimension of depth in life. We saw few tokens of reverence for God or Christ or much interest in the church and the Bible as we grew to maturity. The winning of faith is a rougher proposition for us. We will get started at it later in the day—of that, we may be sure.

A few of us—perhaps more than a few—may have come to a maturity swept clean of faith by some sort of hard experience or other. Bitter about adversity, or conceited over success, or blinded by a little learning, or deeply confused about the meaning of it all, we find ourselves loitering in the market place through most of the days of our life. But when He calls us to enter and work, we have our chance to respond. And it is the chance of a lifetime—our one true opportunity really to live. If we respond and enter and work as best we can to the end of the day, we too may face Him with confident love when the day is done.

God expects us to use all that we are or have in His work. He does not compare what we have or do or give with another. He expects us to give all to Him, all for Him, to lose all in Him—and to await the end of our day and His judgment without fear.

V

Who among us really wants the floor to lift a protest against this? Ought we not rather to rejoice in His generosity, His love to us and to all, and not begrudge it to any? Wordsworth was right!

> Give all thou canst; high heaven rejects the love
> Of nicely-calculated less and more.[3]

Our hope in this life and the next root in one and the same fact: the love of God as we find it in Jesus Christ. In it, we are called to face death and to die. And we are called to do both in confident companionship with the Giver of life eternal. This means more than a continuation of life beyond death; it means new life at once. For it meets us at some deep level of great need in life as we live it now.

It is not necessary to play out our life in a minor key, as some of us do, to crawl tentatively, hesitantly, from one tiny purpose to another like a newly hatched earthworm. The gospel of the love of God is the open door of deliverance from this kind of fearful living, this sort of littleness of life.

Nor is it necessary to go through life reeling under the shock of moral disasters that we or our loved ones may be responsible for or involved in. I am not minimizing the difficulties of meeting this sort of experience. It taxes to the limit every ounce of spiritual energy and courage we can muster. But that is precisely the point of the gospel of the love of God; it is sufficient for even this. No matter where we are or what we have done, it opens the door to a new life for us. In it, by it, and through it we can be freed from the sense of guilt and shame that will distort and can destroy our very lives—we can be freed from them as truly as Mary Magdalene and Matthew and Paul were freed from their sins, and we can walk with confident, loyal, loving courage again.

Let us never say, as once I heard a man say, "Life is just too much for me. I can't take it any longer. It's beaten me down, and I can't get up." Say, if we must, "I haven't the reserves to cope with the challenges that life keeps hurling at me; I just can't meet them any more; I'm going to quit." And that puts the responsibility squarely where it belongs—on us and our unwillingness to let the love of God become the major love of, and power in, our life. The call to enter into His vineyard to labor comes to all, whether early or late; but when it comes we must go in or stay out.

The God whom we see in Jesus Christ is no haggler over details as to when we go in or what we get done. He does not forgive by degrees. He does not dole out His love in a carefully graduated beaker of rewards. He gives it to us—immediately, wholly, overwhelmingly—as we hear and respond to His call to enter His vineyard and work.

The miracle of life—and it is an authentic miracle—is this: The God of the universe can use each one of us—every energy, each relationship and day—in the building of His kingdom of love in the lives of men. Of course this is a universe of moral and spiritual law and order—men of faith have always known that. But there is more to the purposes of God than we have ever been able to reduce to, or express through, laws—and that something more we see in the face of Jesus Christ. He is law lost in love. He is justice fulfilled in love. He is life triumphant over death. To know him is to know God—and to know that God is love.

But to know him is to travel a hard road—as he warned disciples then and now. He does not lead us into a cloister; he takes us to hearthside and market place. We may find him in the sanctuary through worship, but he will take us by the hand and lead us to Gethsemanes and Calvarys of our own in his service. Beyond all these will loom the Easter morn, but we must not separate them. In God's economy, they belong together.

21. Are We Ready for Him?

MATTHEW 25:1-13

I

Preparedness is a word with grim connotations. When we use it, we think of being prepared for the worst. Actually we need to be prepared for the best as well. Our Lord was keenly conscious of this fact and made it the basis of one of his best-known parables, that of the wise and foolish maidens. Like several sister parables, it centers in the wedding ceremonials of Jesus' day—and they seem to have been at least as long, as complicated, and as joyous as the ones we have today.

The nub of the parable is easy to get. The family and the village of the bride are awaiting the arrival of the bridegroom. Etiquette as well as impulse require that he be met outside the village by a procession including some of the bride's close friends, whose special task is to surround him with lights as he makes his way to the home of his beloved. The maidens are there—all ten of them. Half, fearing a delay, have brought extra oil; the rest think they have enough. But the delay occurs and stretches on and on until the girls not only use up the oil in their lamps but fall asleep.

When the cry of his coming is lifted, the ones who have more oil ready their lamps and join the procession. The others finally purchase enough oil to light their lamps again but too late to fulfill their appointed role in the festivities.

The entire point of the parable is contained in the words: "You must be ready, for the son of man is coming at an hour you do not expect." This is a way of saying you must be ready for the best that could happen to you, for the all-important events in your life.

II

This parable helped the early church face and master two crushing disappointments and shattered hopes that might easily have put an end to their movement.

The first was the hope that the Jews would accept Jesus as the long-awaited Messiah. But struggle as those early Apostles, preachers, and missionaries might to achieve this objective, the hope was never fulfilled. While a precious minority of Jews did so accept him, the overwhelming majority did not. It was in answer to this, then, that the notion came into being that God had rejected Israel because Israel rejected Jesus Christ and that God was making of Christians a new Israel, a new people with a New Covenant.

The second frustration of the early church centered in whether, when, and how the risen Lord was going to return to save his people. For the early church, to a man, believed not only that he had risen from the dead and ascended into heaven, but also that he would come again in power and glory to judge the earth, to reward evil doers and righteous ones alike. So far as our records go—and they are scanty enough—the overwhelming consensus of the first Christians seems to have expected an early return. Paul's letters (our earliest New Testament documents) attest to the widespread character of this expectation. The Gospels of Matthew, Mark, and Luke—all written at least a generation after the stirring events of the first Easter—continue to exhibit this strong hope. In Mark we read, "Some of you standing here will not taste death before they see the kingdom of God come with power." The parable of the maidens concludes a long section in the Gospel of Matthew which confidently expects his early return.

Heady hopes die slowly, but this one either had to die or be restated radically because the expected Day of Judgment simply did not come. Christ did not return as expected in the book of Revelation. The early church was faced with the grim alternative of either admitting that the hope was wholly wrong or that it had been misstated.

A grownig body of second, third, and fourth generation Christians went over the entire matter again. They noted several important facts that somehow either had been lost to view or permitted to slip out of focus.

First and all-important was the experience of each Christian that

176HE SPOKE TO THEM IN PARABLES

Christ had really come to him as a personal Savior both saving him from
sin and death and calling him to be one of his witnesses. In a sense,
then, not understood and never to be wholly explained, Christ had already returned to each one of them, in spirit and in truth.

Further, the early Christians felt his presence and power in and
through their fellowship as Christians. He was present at their table;
he was with them in the law courts; he was with them on their lonely
voyages; he was at their side in the deadly arenas. He was not
dwelling in or beyond the clouds awaiting the Day of Judgment—
he was the beating pulse of their common life, their living Lord and
Leader.

"Why," an increasing number of Christian leaders wanted to know
as they rethought the matter of his return, "why spend precious
energy and time wondering whether, when, and how he will return
at some final day when he is the known and experienced Companion
and Lord of our lives even now?"

They believed and preached as the gospel the fact that he stood at
the door of every life and knocked, saying, "If any man hears my
voice and opens the door, I will come in and sup with him and he with
me."

Thus within the church there was and has continued to be a real
difference of opinion on whether he is to come again or has already
returned. We feel some tension on this matter in the deliberations of
the World Council of Churches these days, since a significant number
of Continental theologians seem to be unhappy unless it is affirmed
that "He will come again." Ask them for evidence for this belief, and
you discover that they have no more than that which led the early
Christians to believe in it. You discover that it is an item of faith which
you can neither disprove nor prove by any facts new or old.

Obviously, I must number myself among those who doubt the
wisdom of affirming as an essential item of faith that "He is coming
again" at some future time or moment in history. I know of no reason
to think it; I see no reason to believe it.

But I most emphatically affirm both the reason for believing and the
need to believe that he does stand at the door of every man's life and
seeks entrance, that we need to be prepared for his coming to us, not
once but time and time again as the Lord and Leader of our life. I
subscribe gladly to the statement of faith prepared a few years ago for

use in the United Church of Christ in America. Beginning as all Christian creeds do by centering life and faith in God, the statement continues:

In Jesus Christ, the Man of Nazareth, our crucified and risen Lord, God has come to us, shared our common lot, conquered sin and death, and reconciled the world to himself.

He bestows upon us His Holy Spirit, creating and renewing the Church of Jesus Christ, binding in covenant faithful people of all ages, tongues, and races.

He calls us into His church to accept the cost and joy of discipleship, to be His servants in the service of men, to proclaim the gospel to all the world and resist the powers of evil, to share in Christ's baptism and eat at His table, to join Him in His passion and victory.

He promises, to all who trust Him, forgiveness of sins and fullness of grace, courage in the struggle for justice and peace, His presence in trial and rejoicing, and eternal life in His kingdom which has no end.

Men who believe this and make it the core of their life have too much to do to spend precious time and energy wondering how, when, and whether there is to be a final coming again to the sound of heavenly trumpets. In any event, I am quite sure that the only known way to be prepared for such an eventuality—if it should occur—is to be prepared for the immediate challenge of letting Jesus into our lives here and now.

If, like the early Christians, we open the door of our life to his knock, and invite him to sup with us, what sort of a person will we find him to be?

III

If we may rely on the experiences of those who knew him best and took the trouble to write down those experiences, we may say a number of things with confidence about "our guest."

We will find a man at peace with God and with God's will for his life. He felt called of God to His work, and he had complete faith in God and in the work.

We will find a man at peace with other men—friend, critic, and enemy alike. He neither looked down on sinners and outcasts nor up to the holders of property, prestige, privilege, and power. He heard the crying need for God which existed in all men, and he set himself to answering it. He went among them with the joyous news that he was offering them what they needed above all else: a new relationship with God and a place in the kingdom of God which he was inaugurating.

We will find a man at peace with himself. How could it be otherwise in one who had found peace with God and man? He was inwardly poised and ready for "the slings and arrows of outrageous fortune," for the tricky questions of clever men, for the cruel malice of those who hated him, for the honest blunderings of sincere disciples, for the shallow adoration of the crowd who mistakenly thought he was doing one thing when actually he was doing another. He was so much at peace with God that he never learned to hate his enemies; he never ceased loving all men.

We will find a man who is not buying our ideas about what he ought to say and to do. We will find one whose purpose was his life as well as his message, and we shall find one who expects his followers now as then to make their lives and their message one and the same thing. He has just one reason for seeking entrance into our lives and that is to press the invitation upon us to believe in, to share in, and to become witnesses to the kingdom of God and to help other men prepare for it. If we are not interested in that task, we are not interested in him and his invitation. He gives us a choice—a hard choice, and he knows it—in the invitation to follow him. He knew that no man could hope to follow him without learning the bitter meaning of hard and dangerous living.

IV

I am certain that it would be a mistake for us to try to let him into our lives in any mystical sense unless we are prepared to follow him personally and socially in our day. For his instant and insistent call now as then is "Follow me." What may we expect if we try not only to believe in him as an item of faith, but to follow him as the Lord of our life?

As we follow, we will discover that religious faith is a vital, spontaneous, creative power. It was so with him and those most loyal to him. He was continually confronted by religious people like ourselves whose faith was no longer pliable and growing. Religion so easily settles into certain forms from which it no longer varies and which we no longer question. He ran into that situation repeatedly then, and his living Spirit encounters it now—among and within us.

Recall, if you will, the incident when some criticized him because he let his disciples gather grain for food on the Sabbath day. Such action was against the law of the Sabbath. Jesus answered that the Sabbath was made for man, not man for the Sabbath. To him man and his needs are the most important elements in the situation. For him any expression of faith must be an honest effort to meet the needs of men.

To Jesus religion must be spontaneous enough to relate God to the seemingly insignificant but actually poetic and beautiful elements in life. He seemed to find and to feel the presence of God throughout the whole range of creation. Hence he could speak of God's care for the sparrow, His consideration for the flowers of the field. He could see in the offering of a cup of cold water and in little children, fitting symbols of the proper approach to God. Only one thoroughly alive to the beauty and meaning of commonplace things could see in these the building blocks of great faith. But he did, and he expects those of us who volunteer to follow him to learn to do likewise.

Jesus was not an enemy of form, custom, and convention except as they sought to become the last word in the expression of religious faith. Then he was dead-set against them and never diluted his criticism of them. His faithfulness to the synagogue, the Temple, the holy days of his people, is a well-established fact, and we have no reason to think him hypocritical in his observance of them. He saw them as means to the end of the service of God and never as ends in themselves.

Like our fathers before us, we like to reduce obedience to him to rotelike terms. Charles Sheldon's little book *In His Steps* is a classic example of how we are tempted to do this. Whenever we confront a problem, whether personal or social, we diligently thumb the pages of the Gospel, hoping to find some one utterance of our Lord that will apply. We keep asking, "What would Jesus do?" and vainly strive to answer it from the records. Religion, thus pursued, loses its spontaneity. It becomes barren when we try to use the Gospels as infallible guides to action. As we try this, we are handling our rich religious heritage in the same wooden way that brought the Pharisees under Jesus' disapproval. We ought never to overlook or neglect the fact that Jesus wanted his followers to grow and keep right on growing. He seems to have had unlimited confidence in the continuing power of God in their life and fellowship.

A second emphasis which comes to us as we seek to follow him today is the sheer necessity of believing in God, of being loyal to God as the Lord of our life. God, for Jesus, was all-important. If he experienced normal doubts about the meaning of God, he had worked them through to an affirmative conclusion long before he began his preaching ministry. For, from the moment he steps on the stage of public life, every utterance attributed to him radiates faith in the reality of God and in the kingdom of God as the ultimate goal of the human quest. Hence his proclamation, "The kingdom of God is at hand; prepare ye for it," and his invitation, "If any man would come after me, let him deny himself and take up his cross and follow me."

Clearly, he had a job to do and he wanted helpers—this we must keep in mind if we volunteer to follow him. Yet this kingdom of God of which he spoke was not a delicate dream men could experience by closing their eyes. The God in whom he placed his confidence was striving to create a kingdom which would be characterized by the absence of bitterness, prejudice, hatred, jealousy, and selfishness, and by the presence of gentleness, love, understanding, and co-operation. Jesus never wavered in his insistence that God both stood for this kingdom with every ounce of His will and being, and buoyed up all who strove for it with all their heart, soul, mind, and strength.

He was confident that when the muscles of one who worked for the kingdom wearied in their work, strength not human but divine would pour into them in some mysterious way. He had found it to be so. Why else would he say, "My Father worketh, and I work?" We who would follow him today must be prepared to do more than believe in, and try to find the meaning of, the will of God for human life. We must be ready to devote ourselves wholeheartedly to the fulfillment of it as long as we live.

Still another thing needs to be kept in mind as we seek to be prepared for the one whom we want to hail as our Lord and our Leader this day: Vital loyalty to him must concern itself with the needs of men, personal and social alike. Obviously, this emphasis landed him in serious trouble with the custodians of religion in his time. Many of them seem to have been interested in the minute observance of the law and Temple rituals above all else. At least they had precious little concern over the ordinary needs of ordinary human beings. Jesus handled them with firm hands: "Woe to you, scribes and Pharisees, hypocrites! For you tithe mint and dill and cummin, and have neglected the weightier matters of the law, justice and mercy and faith; these you ought to have done, without neglecting the others. You blind guides, straining out a gnat and swallowing a camel" (Matt. 23:23-24). That's plain enough, and it places the emphasis where prophetic religion has tried to keep it from that day to this: On the abiding ethical concerns of vital religious faith.

Admittedly the church has had a hard time keeping the emphasis there, but we cannot follow Jesus today or any other day without discovering that he leads us into the very depths of human need. And as we follow him, we hear the ancient admonition, "Inasmuch as you have done it unto one of the least of these, my brethren, you have done it unto me."

We are but summing up this emphasis when we say that a Christianity which leaves uncriticized and untouched the personal and social evils of our time is a direct negation of one profound emphasis of vital faith. Creative religion cannot ignore or take an indulgent attitude toward evils based upon the habits of using alcohol, narcotics, and other drugs that weaken and finally destroy a wholesome personality. It will never ignore or treat indulgently the things that make for difficulty in marriage, the home, and the family. It will never stand idly by and let prejudices and bigotry tear the heart out of our society. It will be concerned about the rights of every human being and every group of human beings in our society. One who seeks to follow Jesus today will find himself heavily involved with every major problem that now taxes the minds and the spirits of men.

V

The invitation to be ready to receive Him and to become a follower today is not an invitation to cease thinking and live some kind of lazy intellectual and spiritual life. It is no flight from reality, as some fear; rather it is a serious challenge to summon every energy we now have, to find others we do not now possess, to gird up our capacity for the

mightiest endeavor possible to achieve not only a well-balanced personal
life ourselves, but to work unceasingly at the task of building a decent
world order for all men.

If Christ is literally "the hope of the world" as we say in the easy
parlance of church publications, then let us be clear on the fact that
he must speak to and through people like us. There will be no "angel
visitants," no voice thundering out of the dome of heaven calling instructions to men. Whatever utterance the will of God finds in our time
will be articulated in and through people neither better nor wiser than
we are.

Sometimes I find myself wishing I could revert to my boyhood confidence in miracles. If this were possible, I would lean back and say,
"Let God do it". But since that luxury is denied me, I find myself
compelled to say, "Let God do it—through me, through you, through
the generations yet to come!" Let us be prepared to receive Him as we
find Him in Christ and to be used of Him as were the disciples of old.

Albert Schweitzer uttered words we need to take as food for our
spirit when he said,

He comes to us as One unknown, without a name, by the lake-side. He
came to those men who knew Him not. He speaks to us the same word:
"Follow thou me!" and sets us to the tasks which He has to fulfil for our
time. He commands. And to those who obey Him, whether they be wise
or simple, He will reveal Himself in the toils, the conflicts, the sufferings
which they shall pass through in His fellowship, and, as an ineffable mystery,
they shall learn in their own experiences Who He is.[1]

Is not that reason enough to be ready to receive Him, the Lord and
Savior of our life today?

NOTES

CHAPTER 2. THE POWER OF SMALL THINGS

1. Quoted in *Christian Science Monitor*, Feb. 20, 1958.

CHAPTER 3. THE TOUGHEST TEST MEN FACE

1. *Julius Caesar*, Act III, Scene 2, lines 80-81.
2. From an address by Bertrand Russell, as quoted in the *New York Times*, Nov. 17, 1950.

CHAPTER 4. OH, WE MEAN WELL!

1. Alfred Plummer, *International Critical Commentary: Luke* (New York: Charles Scribner's Sons, 1896), p. 363.
2. W. P. Livingstone, *The Story of David Livingstone* (New York: Harper & Brothers, 1930), pp. 1-2.

CHAPTER 5. PERSISTENCE IS A VIRTUE

1. William Manson, *Gospel of Luke* (New York: Harper & Brothers, 1930), p. 137.
2. Quoted by George A. Buttrick, *The Parables of Jesus* (New York: Harper & Brothers, 1928), p. 174.

CHAPTER 6. OUR DAY OF JUDGMENT

1. *Judaism*, Vols. I, II (Cambridge: Harvard University Press, 1924, 1927).
2. *Ibid.*, Vol. I, p. 332.
3. *The Interpreter's Bible*, Vol. VII (Nashville: Abingdon Press, 1952), p. 562.
4. Quoted in *Ibid.*, p. 563.

CHAPTER 8. DEVILS LOVE A VACUUM

1. From "The Second Coming," *Collected Poems* (New York: The Macmillan Company, 1933). Used by permission of the publisher.
2. Quoted in Halford E. Luccock and Frances Bretano (eds.), *The Questing Spirit* (New York: Coward-McCann, 1947), p. 37.

CHAPTER 9. WANTED: SPECIAL MESSENGERS!

1. Shakespeare. Act III, Scene 4, lines 28-32.
2. Louis F. Benson. Used by permission of Mrs. Robert E. Jefferys.

CHAPTER 10. HOW BLIND CAN WE BE?

1. "Be Strong," *Thoughts for Everyday Living* (New York: Charles Scribner's Sons, 1901).

2. James Dalton Morrison (ed.), *Masterpieces of Religious Verse* (New York: Harper & Brothers, 1948).

3. Willard L. Sperry, *Prayers for Private Devotions in War-Time* (New York: Harper & Brothers, 1943), p. 9.

CHAPTER 11. THE WORD AND THE DEED

1. New York: The John Day Company, 1943, p. 158.

CHAPTER 12. THE POWER TO RECEIVE GREAT THINGS

1. *A Testament of Devotion* (New York: Harper & Brothers, 1941), p. 3.

2. "Sleeveless Errand" by Elise S. Peckham, *Saturday Review*, Vol. XXXII, No. 48, p. 45. Used by permission of the publisher.

3. Learned Hand, *The Spirit of Liberty* (New York: Alfred A. Knopf, 1953), p. 190.

CHAPTER 13. GOD'S ULTIMATUM TO MAN

1. Henry C. Link, *The Return to Religion* (New York: The Macmillan Company, 1936), p. 95.

2. New York: Charles Scribner's Sons, 1950, p. 146.

CHAPTER 14. WHERE CHRISTIANITY BEGINS

1. *The Souls of Black Folk* (London: Archibald Constable & Co., 1905), pp. 226-27.

CHAPTER 15. SHALL WE BE PATIENT WITH EVIL?

1. Learned Hand, *The Spirit of Liberty* (New York: Alfred A. Knopf, 1953), pp. 256-57.

CHAPTER 18. "THE GOD OF THE LOST"

1. *The Synoptic Gospels*, Vol. II (2nd ed.; London: Macmillan and Co., 1927), pp. 520-21.

2. From "Foreign Missions in Battle Array," *Collected Poems* (New York: The Macmillan Company, 1925). Used by permission of the publisher.

CHAPTER 19. HONORED BY GOD

1. *The New Testament in the Light of Modern Research* (Garden City, N.Y.: Doubleday, Doran & Company, 1929), *passim.*

CHAPTER 20. THE GENEROSITY OF GOD

1. Shakespeare, *Hamlet*, Act II, Scene 2, lines 519-22.

2. Act IV, Scene 1, lines 192-99.

3. From "Ecclesiastical Sonnets," XLIII.

CHAPTER 21. ARE WE READY FOR HIM?

1. *The Quest of the Historical Jesus* (3rd ed.; London: Adam & Charles Black, 1954), p. 401.